# Swimming with Frogs

# Swimming with Frogs

## Life in the Brown County Hills

## Ruth Ann Ingraham

AN IMPRINT OF

INDIANA UNIVERSITY PRESS

BLOOMINGTON AND INDIANAPOLIS

This book is a publication of

Indiana University Press
601 North Morton Street
Bloomington, IN 47404-3797 USA

http://iupress.indiana.edu

*Telephone orders*   800-842-6796
*Fax orders*   812-855-7931
*Orders by e-mail*   iuporder@indiana.edu

Manufactured in the United States of America

Library of Congress Cataloging-in-Publication Data

Ingraham, Ruth Ann.
  Swimming with frogs : life in the Brown County hills /
Ruth Ann Ingraham.
      p. cm.
  Includes bibliographical references and index.
  ISBN 0-253-34543-x (cloth : alk. paper) —
  ISBN 0-253-21756-3 (pbk. : alk. paper)
  1. Natural history—Indiana—Brown County.
  2. Country life—Indiana—Brown County. I Title.
  QH105.I6I55 2005
  508.772'253—dc22                    2004013325
1 2 3 4 5 10 09 08 07 06 05

I dedicate this book to the memory of
*Joseph Sterling Ingraham* and
place its spirit and message into the
hands of our grandchildren—

Connor Scott Gable

Rosalie Estelle Lawrence

Flora Lyra Lawrence

Sarah Judith Ingraham

David Loring Ingraham

# Contents

# In Gratitude

SO MANY HAVE MADE IT possible for me to reach this pinnacle. In gratitude I thank these people.

Joseph Ingraham, my beloved husband for our all-too-brief eight years, unreservedly believed in me. A practitioner of the "art of loving," he pointedly did everything he could to enable me to be the best at whatever I chose, and he predicted that I would do "great things" after he was gone. May this book partially fulfill his vision.

Lois and Clarence Cornish, my parents, revered learning and sought out beauty. Even into the tenth decade of their lives, they continued to photograph our nation's vast scenic splendors as well as nature's minute and intricate forms. They left me a legacy.

Lisa Krieg and Christy Krieg, my two fabulous daughters, ride the waves with me—and I with them. They cherish what I cherish, and because of that, they give me a profound sense of comfort and hope.

Mike Gable inspired the title for this book.

June Loomis, my nearest Brown County neighbor, suggested several years before I first put fingers to keyboard that I write a book about my observations of Brown County life. Her encouragement never wavered.

Ruth Ann Schmitt, my Chicago friend, volunteered to read and critique the manuscript. Her legal background led to pertinent questions cushioned by encouraging comments as she nudged me into the final phase of my book—having it formally edited.

Alice Vollmar, Minneapolis friend and author, coached me on ways to make my writing "sparkle" by adding more descriptive words.

Tom and Bernie Zoss are my mentors who never doubted, even when I did, that this book would be a reality. They made crucial recommendations along the way.

Jim Diehl, Bobbi Diehl, and Sue McConnell, Bobbi's Canadian cousin, read the first lengthy, awkward text as well as the second of what would be multiple versions, and made vital comments.

When I felt most discouraged, Scott Watson, Director of the Writer's Center of Indianapolis, and Mark Shaw, author and Director of the Books For Life Foundation, insisted that I not give up and helped me move forward.

Many gave their time and intellect to review paragraphs and, in some cases, several chapters related to their fields of expertise:

Mike Lannoo, Ph.D., Neuroscientist, Muncie Center for Medical Education

Jim Eagleman, Naturalist, Brown County State Park

Lee Casebere, Assistant Director, Division of Nature Preserves, Indiana Department of Natural Resources

Dan Shaver, Director, The Nature Conservancy, Brown County Hills Project

Mike Homoya, Botanist/Plant Ecologist, Division of Nature Preserves, Indiana Department of Natural Resources

Donald G. Ruch, Ph.D., Associate Professor of Biology, Ball State University

Stan Riggs, Ph.D., Emeritus Professor of Geology, East Carolina University

Cathy Paradise, District Coordinator, Brown County Soil and Water Conservation

Robert Waltz, Ph.D., Indiana State Entomologist

James W. Atkinson, Professor of Zoology, Michigan State University

Jim Mitchell, Deer Biologist, Indiana Department of Natural
  Resources

Spencer Cortwright, Associate Professor, Department of Biology,
  Indiana University Northwest

James E. Lloyd, Ph.D., Emeritus Professor of Entomology and
  Nematology, University of Florida

Arthur R. Zangerl, Ph.D., Senior Research Scientist, Insect-Plant
  Interactions, University of Illinois

Authors Robert Pyle, Ann Zwinger, Tim McNulty, and William
Dietrich, my instructors at a Nature Writer's Retreat sponsored by
the North Cascades Institute, challenged, educated, and inspired me.

These words of an acquaintance, "You'll get it done; you always
do," never left me.

I thank fellow members of the Indiana Native Plant and Wildflower
Society who magnanimously share their knowledge and teach me continuously about our plant life.

I could not have written this book without the myriad authors
who, through their own labors and books, preceded me and answered
my need to know more.

My longtime friends the Birthday Girls—Jan, Marni, Jane, Jenny,
Judy, Anne, Kris, Connie, and Sarah—may have disbelieved at first
but then believed and now await their signed copies.

Friend and artist Chris Carlson has gone far beyond the simple
pen and ink sketches that I envisioned to create the appealing drawings that introduce each chapter.

I thank Pamela Rude, designer, who gave this book the look and
feel that I had hoped for.

Finally, I thank Jane Nolan, who led me to Jane Lyle, my skillful, gentle editor, who, when I could do no more, allowed me the luxury of transferring my manuscript into her care. You, the readers, will have a smoother experience because of Jane's sensitive work.

# Swimming with Frogs

# Prologue

The important thing is to start:
to lay a plan, and then follow it
step by step no matter how small or
large each one by itself may seem.

—CHARLES LINDBERGH

BROWN COUNTY, INDIANA, and other sparsely inhabited, predominantly natural areas will be different places in twenty-five, fifty, or one hundred years, just as most are vastly different now from what they were fifty, one hundred, and especially two hundred years ago, prior to the arrival of European settlers. I hope that my experiences in a tiny portion of Brown County, recorded during the final decade of the final century of the second millennium AD and the beginning of the third and assimilated into this book, will be of interest now and into the future.

I began keeping journals on December 12, 1990. In them I wrote about weather, rainfall, birds, flowers, visitors, menus, games, swims, skiing, television shows, hikes, neighbors, deer, mice, workmen, cisterns, woodstoves, the sky, the stars and planets, insects, snakes, the pond, my feelings for my husband Joe, his labors, and our love. Would any of this matter to others? I wondered. Then I read *Writing Past Dark* by Bonnie Friedman, who states, "We are all bodies in the world, and our stories are the stories of bodies. To write meaningfully, we must grasp that. And that is all we must grasp. This is marvelous news! . . . This is why people read: to have experiences. We have all had experiences. . . . If they are profound to us, we can make them profound to a reader, but it takes work: we must let the reader see what we saw, touch what we touched, hear what we thought and felt. To see an ordinary thing clearly is highly unusual."

Joe Ingraham died in 1997, and Cassie, the canine companion who had been with me for fourteen years, died three years later. I entered a solitary, reflective phase and resolved to write about nature, survival, regeneration, giving back, and love; about what I gleaned from being silent, listening, touching, seeing, and absorbing; and about discovering the magnificent diversity revealed when Brown County's multicolored panoply of leaves is peeled back. How could I have known in 1990, when Joe and I purchased a simple little cabin with a few acres of land, how much this bit of earth and its accoutrements would penetrate my soul, and how it would clarify what I care about and stand for?

Looking back to the mid-1950s, I remember high school composition as a tough subject. Writing assignments were daunting. I would sit at the Formica-topped breakfast table that took up most of the floor space in our tiny kitchen and stare at the blank sheet of paper that awaited the required 300 *bons mots*. I counted them one by one—10 down and 290 to go; if I was lucky, 290 down and 10 to go. So how did I leap from that repressed, nascent stage to the 100,000 words that I had to tighten and trim for this book? Two words—practice and passion.

Practice began in 1963, when, while on the adventure of a lifetime, I kept a detailed diary. My new husband, Peter Krieg, and I crossed the Atlantic Ocean on a German freighter and moved into a Volkswagen Kombi camper, which would be our home on wheels for the next nine months and get us through the Sahara Desert on a sand and gravel piste, or track. Twenty-four years later, as I deliberately moved out of one mode and entered into the uncertainty and unknown of another, I wrote in a letter to our daughter Lisa, who was in Europe: "It is reminiscent of crossing the Straits of Gibraltar at night, leaving Europe behind and landing in Africa. We were scared. Where would we sleep? How would we find food? How would we be treated by these strange people? Would we be harmed? Would we survive? Of course, the African adventure, rough as it was, turned out to be one of the most significant character-forming elements of my life."

Practice continued with my Brown County journals. Often I had difficulty transcribing rough notes into a coherent whole in my blank books. Then I read John McPhee's *Words from the Land*. He said to a questioner at the Princeton YMCA, "I'll tell you how to get started. You put a piece of paper in the typewriter and type: Dear Mother, I am having an awful time trying to begin a piece of writing. It just won't work. It's wretched. It's dreadful. You see, it has to do with a certain grizzly bear in northwest Alaska. I can't do it. It's awful. This bear was standing on the hillside eating blueberries. . . . Keep on writing about the bear. Then keep going. Then go back and cut off the Dear Mother and all that garbage at the beginning. And there you are. You've gotten somewhere." Substituting the names of my daughters or friends, I found that this method actually worked for me.

The moment of truth arrived on January 16, 2001. I had reread my journal and listed, in a spreadsheet, more than three hundred topics and their page references. I was ready to begin. Or was I? I made three attempts to write page one. Ah, the crux of it was that I managed to avoid getting started. I washed a small number of dishes and even dried them. I scoured the porcelain sink to get rid of imagined stains. I shoveled snow, which was melting in the sun, from the decks. Then I pulled *Bird by Bird* by Anne Lamott from my bookshelf. A writer and teacher of writing, she advises: "do a short assignment and don't worry about doing it well, just get it down. . . . The core, ethical concepts in which you most passionately believe are the language in which you are writing." I began by writing about that life-sustaining commodity—water. Three years later, I completed the task of writing this book.

Ann Riggs, my Beloit College roommate in the mid-fifties and now from eastern North Carolina, described her impression of my Brown County retreat. Coming on gravel roads, she felt she had stepped back in time into quiet isolation with dark nights. She wrote, "It's a comfortable, wild place, not awesome in the sense of overly rugged or inaccessible. An inviting wildness." Join me.

# *Summertime*

All creatures, however insignificant,
are intelligent about their own
affairs—just like people.

—ETSU INAGAKI SUGIMOTO

I ARRIVED AT THE CABIN with my husband Joe on a July evening. An urgent, repeated call rose from the valley: "Kee-yer," repeated five, six, seven times, every few minutes, ascending to a shrieked conclusion. I believed that the bird was a juvenile red-shouldered hawk. The cries ended at sundown and resumed at sunrise. Curious, I walked down with Cassie, my dog. We approached the opening to the meadow with utmost caution, in time to glimpse the large bird turn and swoop into the trees on the far side. We sat on the mowed path in the shade and waited; I hoped to see it again.

Eventually, the juvenile hawk emerged and flew onto a bare branch twenty feet above ground. It preened its feathers, turned its head to look up and down, and called, "I'm here I'm hungry Don't forget me I'm hungry I'm here," before flying to the far end of the meadow. From the distance came an infrequent, barely audible response, as though saying, "I know Patience I'll return." I wanted to satisfy my maternal instincts and see the bird fed, so we waited half an hour or so longer. However, the young hawk vanished into the forest, alarmed when I stood up for a better look at a white-tailed deer that had bounded across the meadow with its tail in straight-up alert. Branches snapped under the deer's hooves as it vanished in the forest's undergrowth.

Cassie stayed with me for a leisurely walk while I checked on things. Cassie was a shepherd mix that my family had selected from dozens of dogs (and cats) at the Noblesville Home for Friendless Animals in 1986. Her fur was the color of honey-brown oak, lightly brushed with black. Her tail? She didn't really have one. What she had instead was a two-inch stump—a curiosity especially for children. "What happened to your dog's tail?" they would ask earnestly. We didn't have an answer, although we knew that she had been mistreated during the first year of her life. Eventually she lost her debilitating fear of our basement stairs and dark spaces, but she never lost her fear of people dressed in dark clothing. Cassie was our loving, devoted companion until the heart-rending day in 2000 when she died.

Before we left the meadow and entered into the forest, a pair of scarlet tanagers alighted slightly above my eye level in a small grove of tall sumacs, the male's black wings in stunning, crisp contrast to his crimson body. When we arrived at the ephemeral creek that meanders through the forest, tiny fish dashed for cover under stone ledges and into shadowy spaces around the edges of isolated pools, where long-legged, wiry water striders cast darting shadows on the gravel beneath. Beyond a grove of spicebush, a graceful understory shrub that produces shiny red berries that were ground by early settlers for allspice, I found a twayblade orchid plant, its single flower stalk embellished with small, upright seedpods. I skirted the crown of a fallen tree and stepped over musty, rotting logs to revisit a patch of green violets with their relatively oversized seedpods. A green violet, unlike its familiar showy relatives, can grow more than a yard tall and produces tiny green blossoms in the leaf axils.

Joe and I had introduced a skunk cabbage at the edge of the creek bed and had enclosed it with fencing, not knowing whether it would be a savory treat for deer or not. The protected plant was alive, but the foliage had been grossly chewed by insects, not by deer. Skunk cabbages grow in seeps and moist places. They produce sufficient heat to melt the snow from around them as early as February, when they bloom in central Indiana. Blooming nearby were lizard tails, which we had also introduced and fenced. Following a groove carved by rushing water during heavy rains, Cassie and I arrived at one of the areas where sweeps of pale orange chanterelles with flared stalks burst forth midsummer near delicate swirls of maidenhair ferns.

We followed the base of the sedge-covered hillside and then cut up to look at fern-leafed false foxglove plants. Those that Joe and I had fenced were fine. The tips of the unprotected ones, which would have produced flowers, had been eaten. Deer again. I rested on the hillside under high boughs of beech and oak trees, using pillow-like clumps of sedges and thick drifts of dry leaves as cushions. My beautiful dog sat a few feet away, patiently waiting for me to decide where we would go next.

Glancing around me, I noticed examples of a feature of our woods—pits and mounds. I recently learned from the American Native Plant Society in Ontario that pits and mounds form after large trees are torn from the ground during violent storms. The pits are created where the roots are wrenched from the earth, leaving large craters. The mounds form more slowly: when the doomed trees fall, their root masses drag a hill of topsoil mixed with subsoil along with them. The roots then rot down over a couple of decades, leaving a mound beside a pit where the tree once stood. The resulting topography can help to maintain forest biodiversity, with the mounds and pits providing niches for a wide variety of plants and wildlife.*

Rested, Cassie and I headed toward the dam. On the way I noted another new-to-me plant, a vine that spread along the ground with clover-like leaves the size of quarters. Prostrate tick trefoil, I later learned. From the dam I watched largemouth bass target a school of small fish. Damselflies and dragonflies, some with wings the

---

*This natural topography has been mimicked in an Ontario reforestation project. At the end of a construction day, stormwater flowed across the newly configured ground of a former soybean field and pooled in the pits, followed that night by an army of spring peepers, American toads, and leopard frogs that moved in from the surrounding forest and filled the night air with a deafening chorus. By morning the water-filled pits were teeming with the egg masses of amphibians.

color of polished copper and others with wings banded in black and milky blue, darted and hovered above the pond's surface. Dozens of tiny blue darners flitted erratically.

Cassie and I had been looking things over long enough. It was time to head back up the old log drag to the cabin. Being careful not to squash the tiny toads that leapt in every direction, I stopped at the sharp bend in the path to account for all four of the cranefly orchid flower stalks that grow on a small rise. Lastly, amid ferns and club moss, I plucked a handful of tart low-bush blueberries, my gift to Joe for his lunch.

That afternoon the hammock invited me to take a long, but hot, nap. Then a strong thunderstorm passed through. As it did, the plants in the tall grass hedge swayed violently in unison; birdlike leaves flew with the invisible force; and drenching rain refreshed. Twenty degrees' worth of oppressive air was swept away and replaced with cooler, lighter air. Clear skies with silver-white wisps of clouds inspired me to return to the woods in search of mushrooms, new flowers, and the juvenile hawk, heard only occasionally after that morning.

Rosalie and Flora, two of Joe's four grandchildren, have spent parts of many summers here. The nearest body of water to their California home is the Pacific Ocean, a mere three streets away. Yet when they arrive in Brown County, my little pond is an instant magnet for swims with tickling tadpoles. The creek runs with clear pools where they can wade, float, and, from crouched positions or on their bellies, rearrange creek gravel to make channels and harbors for the wood block boats made from scrap lumber salvaged by their mom, Joe's daughter, Mary Edith. Back at the cabin, giggling,

tickling, and teasing each other, they swing in the hammock before
running back to the woods to examine tiny toads, and then back up
again to watch inchworms measuring their weary way along the
railing or catch a glimpse of a rarely seen nymphal stage of a praying mantis. They cool off from Indiana's summertime heat in a
"cloudburst" from the hose, fill in drawings of flowers in a coloring book that match those blooming in the meadow, pick blueberries, build imaginary structures with original Tinker Toys, learn to
peel apples (without a break in the peel), and try to identify birds,
trees, insects, and frogs.

Cope's gray treefrogs were vocal and loud one night when the
girls were here, so Rosalie and I went on a frog hunt. We were
surrounded by frogs among the shrubs and foliage that grow around
the pond, but at first we didn't spot one. We didn't give up, though,
and eventually we found two in mating position on the cane of a
multiflora rose. The female impressed us when she jumped away to
another cane with the male hanging on for the ride. Back in the
cabin, Rosalie called her dad, who had stayed in California, to share
with him what she had witnessed.

Connor, my then four-year-old grandson from Pittsburgh, stayed
at "Gramma's Cabin" for a couple of days. He and I slept in my
tent staked down on a hard-to-find level space near the cabin. A
gentle-looking moon giant peered over the horizon as we crawled
into the tent. Calls of frogs and a whippoorwill were the last sounds
we heard before drifting to sleep.

June, July, and August—Brown County's summer months—
support heat, birth, and growth. In the early part of our hottest
months, songs of courting birds waken you before dawn; after dusk,

firefly larvae, called glowworms by some, produce a sluggish on-again, off-again cool light on the ground until, as winged adults, they take flight and add their magic to the night air. Darkness is naturally noisy with whippoorwills, owls, flying squirrels, frogs, toads, and, later in the season, crickets and katydids. Gold, yellow, iridescent, and black butterflies tickle the days. Tadpoles, turtles, and fish are your swimming companions. Chanterelle mushrooms and Indian pipes erupt. Though I curse the heat and yell that it's too sultry, horrible, stifling, oppressive, miserable, hot and humid, hot and dry, and parched, I praise moments of sweet relief with the words best, exquisite, heavenly, cool, chilly, glorious, idyllic, perfect, wonderful, or sensually pleasant.

I waited one evening by the pond and communed with nature. Waited for what? Anything. A secretive Louisiana waterthrush, often heard late in the day, flew into a shrub at the edge of the pond and chipped, its rear end distinctively bobbing. A male scarlet tanager streaked directly across from the valley to the blueberry bush behind me, from which, moments before, I had plucked a few. Then I heard what had begun to be a familiar sound of dusk, a faint hum which, when I cupped my hands behind my ears, grew and seemed quite significant. Was it created by the awakening of hundreds of thousands of nocturnal insects?

In late June, beginning around 7:45 PM and continuing for an hour when the whippoorwill began, the ovenbird "sang" its crescendoing *teach-teach-teach-teach* from the deeply shaded woods south of the dam. Its flights through the understory vegetation were invisible to me; its ghostly form eluded me even though I stood quietly for ten or fifteen minutes only ten or fifteen feet away from it.

Turning around, I watched a rather large pinkish-tan bat with powdery dark wings dip its mouth several times into the pond while in the straight-as-an-arrow flight that took it into the darkening ravine. Later, two smaller, darker bats appeared out of nowhere, circling and dipping silently. I sat undetected by a raccoon that toddled out of the woods and down the far slope to sip from the pond. A deer that approached from behind and above saw me, stomped its feet over and over, and then bounded away, snorting its displeasure. A few feet from my toe tips, two-inch-long banded fish swished around under a small, flat stone, stirring up the mud, while further out, a painted turtle floated with its snout sticking out of the water. Frogs lunged in with a plop. How was I feeling? Utterly contented. I could close every day at the pond. And when I think about not being alive to experience that tranquility ad infinitum, I feel sad. It's unimaginable. When it was nearly dark, I reluctantly left, stopping briefly in the darkening, mystical forest sprinkled with flashes of firefly light.

Most plants peak by or in August and begin their decline. September connects summer to fall. Oaks, beeches, maples, and hickories remain summer-green while dogwoods and sumacs turn apple-red. Days are warm and nights chilly. I stroke the fuzziness of somnolent bumblebees where they remain latched to flower heads on cold mornings, awaiting the sun's warmth.

Grasshoppers, their songs pervasive all night long, mate and deposit eggs in the ground to overwinter. Angular green katydids cling to screens day and night, startling me with their tropical, rasping sounds. Once I watched as two band-winged grasshoppers, their hind wings brightly colored, leapt straight up three and four feet, hovered with a soft whirring sound, and settled back to earth. They aligned themselves side by side on the drive and, for several minutes, repeatedly and slowly raised and lowered their hind legs, one leg and sometimes both together. Was this body language or calisthenics?

The curtain slowly draws closed. Most plants and animals have had their chance to successfully reproduce their DNA (as Joe put it) or not. The reproductive year becomes history, and seven months must pass before the make-or-break opportunity begins anew.

# Transitions

I HAVE MULTIPLE GOOD FORTUNES—my daughters, my grandson, Joe's children and four grandchildren, our excellent health, an extended family of friends, abundant interests and concerns, gardens, and all the books I choose to be surrounded with. Additionally, I am blessed with a home nestled in Broad Ripple, a bustling neighborhood in the northern part of Indianapolis, and a cabin tucked into the inviting wildness of scenic south-central Indiana, where I spend around a quarter of each year. The lineal distance between these two places is sixty-five miles; the spiritual distance is immeasurable.

The most expeditious way to the cabin from Broad Ripple is via Keystone Avenue and major highways. Keystone, primarily a commercial strip, is lined with car dealerships, fast food chains, and some small businesses. Halfway from my house to I-70, mouth-watering aromas from King Ribs Bar-B-Q drift into my car and linger as I whiz, within a car's length, past blocks of post–World War II aluminum-sided bungalows and then an elementary school, a Quik Cash, a pawnshop, and the Marion County Juvenile Detention Center. Then my Subaru instinctively curves up to I-70, where, with sweaty palms tensely gripping the steering wheel, I cross four lanes of dense, hurtling traffic in order to head south. Indianapolis's burgeoning center moves past like a film in slow motion as I maneuver again to merge onto I-65, which leads me, forty miles ahead, to State Road 46 and the final fifteen-mile leg of the journey.

Signs that point to Brown County State Park and children's camps also indicate my turn toward Clay Lick, a now-paved road that follows the creek where my best grade-school friend and I built dams, and the hillside where we collected moss for terrariums. Bluebird boxes dot the shoulder, and one of Brown County's picturesque farms comes into view. As I angle onto Wallow Hollow, gravel pings against the underside of my car. Almost there! After the second bridge, I shift down to second gear for the steep slope, after which the road flattens out and snakes along the ridge to my ninefoot-tall gate, part of a deer exclusion fence.

I step out, exhale the city's scent, and inhale nature's aromatic blend of earth, trees, grasses, and flowers. My routine kicks in— unlock the cabin, unload the car, flick on the breakers for the water pump and water heater, transfer cold foods to the refrigerator, fill the bird feeders, and, in winter, start a fire. In summer I carry a glass of chilled Sauvignon Blanc or Chardonnay to the deck. There, with my feet propped on the rail, I make the final shift from city to country—a slow and quiet immersion.

"Hope you enjoy *Gift from the Sea* as much as I have," Roger Cox,

a family friend, wrote in the 1965 paperback edition he gave me
long ago. The acidic pages are yellow-brown, yet Anne Morrow
Lindbergh's wisdom is legible. With a moon shell held in her hand
she wrote, "On its smooth symmetrical face is penciled with preci-
sion a perfect spiral, winding inward to the pinpoint center of the
shell, the tiny dark core of the apex. . . . it is an island set in ever-
widening circles of waves, alone, self-contained, serene." I read that
passage one February day when dense fog settled around the cabin
and obscured the view down and beyond the pond to the valley
and Annie's Ridge. Surrounded by a curtain of moist white air, I
felt centered on an island of serene space.

We bought this cabin and acreage in 1990. Joe had retired from
more than thirty years as professor with the Indiana University
School of Medicine, Department of Immunology and Microbiology. I was Executive Director of Offender Aid and Restoration of
Marion County (OAR), a not-for-profit agency in Indianapolis
that worked with men and women in and out of the county's jail.
My work was demanding; I needed serenity, and Brown County
gave me that. At first, Joe and I would stay in Indianapolis to do
Saturday morning chores before heading for the cabin, arriving early
in the afternoon. We drove back up on Sunday evenings. A day and
a half was not enough, so we abandoned Saturday chores, and Joe
began picking me up on Fridays after work. That wasn't enough
either, so we found ourselves delaying and making rushed departures Monday mornings, leaving barely enough minutes back in
Indianapolis for me to shower, don my administrative garb, and
make it to my downtown office by 9:00 AM.

Our early motto for this place had been "All play and no work,"
but we did both. Some friends built a large house of native wood

and stone in the eastern part of Brown County. Their retreat was for rest and relaxation only, and they arranged for their firewood to be cut, split, and piled by the fireplace prior to their arrival. They laughed when we described loading cut logs into our wheelbarrow below the cabin, wrapping a rope tied to the wheelbarrow around my waist, and, as I pulled and Joe pushed, hauling it up to our wood pile. If not good exercise, work seemed like play. I transplanted wildflowers from my mother's garden, harvested fern-leafed false foxglove and bittersweet seeds and scattered them in new locations, and made spicebush leaf tea and dandelion beer from recipes in *Wild Food* by Roger Phillips. (Although the beer didn't ferment, I had fun trying.) Joe, who craved physical busyness, had never-ending lists of projects. Like the ice crystals on a sunny day under the scrutiny of our pocket microscope, time melted away, gone before it had begun, it seemed. We relaxed, explored, discovered something new each visit, and relished simple pleasures.

While in Brown County, thoughts of my professional duties and obligations evaporated until work pressures began to cast a fifty-five-mile shadow. In the spring of 1992, I resigned from OAR. I was free to enjoy life more fully with Joe and to give more attention to my parents, who were then in their nineties.

But what about Brown County, my weekend retreat, my former getaway from work-related pressures? Now what would its purpose be? Could I justify deep immersion in this environment with boundless time to look, listen, absorb, and photograph insects, fungi, and meadow flowers? Justified or not, Joe and I reveled in it. The sun had long since set on a cool, cloudless fall evening. Suppertime was overdue. It would be a simple one—mashed butternut squash and lightly cooked apple chunks spiked with orange juice, and on the side, my version of stir-fried rice. But as I walked into the kitchen, I glimpsed the waning sliver of moon through our back window and called to Joe, "Turn the lights off and join me on the back deck. We can't miss this moment." The moon, with a bright planet suspended to its left, shone above the hemlocks. Leaning into one another, we mentally pinched ourselves to be sure that our being there for such simple, stellar moments was real.

We continued to happily share our mutual discoveries of small wonders with family and friends—the cool luminescence of a firefly larva that grows and fades, grows and fades; eerie bioluminescent mushrooms that emit a faint light in the dark on long-dead wood; tiny black froglets that mass, ready to cross from water to land. Our observations bred questions: Why are grasshoppers, praying mantises, walkingsticks, and katydids abundant some years and sparse others? How soon will plants and animals repopulate the pond after the dam is demolished and rebuilt? What will emerge from earth turned topsy-turvy by the bulldozer? Why does the cardinal still sing in the fall after courting season is over? Why are persimmons sometimes not ripe in November when in other years they fall, soft and delectable, in late September? Is it coincidental that pink wild geraniums, yellow zigzag goldenrods, and blue asters grow in abundant numbers inside the deer exclusion fence and are stunted to nonexistent immediately outside?

This place served as a peaceful retreat when my life became otherwise clouded. My parents died within six months of one another, in 1995 and 1996. The sad and daunting task of sorting their lifetime accumulation of furnishings, clothing, and artifacts became mine, and it depleted me. An obstreperous tenant in the house that was mine to manage in Broad Ripple tested my patience. Ur-

ban sprawl growing southward from Indianapolis gnawed into my
aesthetic and environmental sense. The diminished look of logged
woodlands north of us in Brown County depressed me. But when
I arrived at the cabin and stepped from the car, the clouds evaporated. The sounds of burbling stream, birds, and frogs greeted me.
With no mail, no computer (then), no daily newspaper, no laundry
facilities, little clutter, and few outside demands, I stepped into a
simple, protected, and soothing life.

About the same time, in the mid-'90s, I asked, "Joe, if something happened to me, where would you live?" His answer was that
he would live here permanently and set up a shop for woodworking
and ceramics. Joe had been diagnosed with prostate cancer that was
being treated, so the question had the poignant ring of reality when
I asked myself where I would live without him. Could I manage
two homes by myself? Could I leave my Indianapolis home of
thirty years and the neighborhood where I had lived for fifty years?
Would I give up social diversity for biodiversity? My assumption
then was that I could not manage two residences and that I would
sell the cabin, even though it and the surrounding land had become
the centerpiece of my life with Joe. In 1997, seven years after Joe
and I became stewards here, he died. The question I had asked
myself a few years earlier and my response no longer applied. I
could not let go of either my Brown County retreat or my Indianapolis home. I cared about and, fortunately, could manage both.

My Broad Ripple neighborhood offers easy access to the popular Monon Trail, as well as a lively and trendy mix of restaurants,
shops, bars, and live entertainment at its center. Nighttime activities sometimes spill onto my neighborhood streets, and peace can
be elusive. Understandably, I thrive amid the quiet that predomi-

nates here at the cabin in Brown County. During an interview on the Indiana University radio station, WFIU-FM, composer Arvo Part spoke about interludes of quiet in his music. Those interludes are as important as sound, he said: "Silence is to experience inner quietness." There are times when, as intently as I listen, I hear not even the sound of a rustling leaf. Such moments are ephemeral and precious. Then, in the dark, I lean against the deck's railing, rest my chin in my cupped hands, and listen again. Sounds rise from water purling down to Cassie Creek from the pond, invertebrates rustling under leaf litter, and a green frog calling for a mate, as does a distant whippoorwill. In this inviting wildness, darkness is sprinkled with celestial light, and silence is interspersed with nature's sounds.

I live nearly every waking moment here alert to the possibility of a new bird or a new insect—or at least one I've not seen for months or years—or that an infrequent visitor, even a squirrel or a chipmunk, will stop at the shallow watering dish on the rail for a refreshing sip. Birds—what a lure they are. Stay a little longer, I say to myself. There may be a reward. Today a cerulean; tomorrow a prothonotary? I may find it impossible to justify leaving—even though I've stayed a day longer than planned. When I finally close the cabin, climb into my car, turn up the drive, and head back to the city and the transition to my other world, I always wonder what will happen while I'm gone—sorry that I will not know.

> Look, I want to love this world
> as though it's the last chance I'm ever going to get
> to be alive
> and know it.
> —Mary Oliver, *"October"*

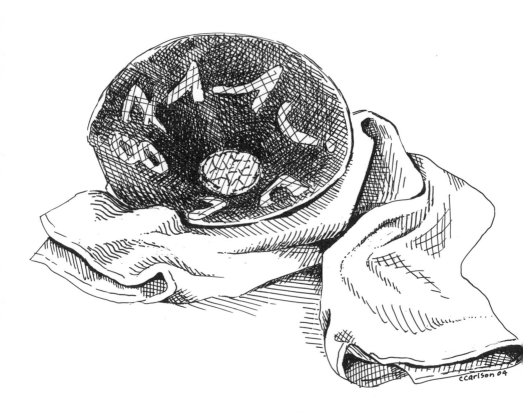

# *Idyll*

IT WASN'T NATURE that first connected Joe and me. It was Liao, a cultural exchange participant from Anhui, China, who can take credit for that twist of fate. Unknown to each other, Joe and I had both volunteered to house Liao for part of his yearlong stay in Indianapolis. On July 11, 1987, after Liao had been my houseguest for five weeks, I drove him to his next host, Dr. Ingraham.

My first husband, Peter Krieg, and I were separating after twenty-six years of marriage, and on that same July day, mutual friends helped move Peter's family heirlooms—including the dining room chairs and the living room desk—to the nearby house where he would live. Saturday, July 11, 1987, was a pivotal day—the symbolic close to a long and in many ways rewarding marriage, and the opening of a new relationship that would blossom and flourish.

Joe and I met again at some social events organized for all the international participants and host families. We soon discovered that we both enjoyed gardening and classical music. An invitation to join Joe for an Indianapolis Symphony Orchestra performance ensued. Not long after that, I decided to stop by his house after work to inquire whether he had found the loaf of zucchini bread that I had left at his door that morning. Joe, this considerably older man, was out back in his gardening attire, tending his vegetable garden, where Swiss chard, Brussels sprouts, kohlrabi, and parsnips grew among tomatoes and sweet corn, and Chinese beans climbed strings up the side of his garage. I said, "If you're having a glass of wine before dinner, I'll join you." He didn't refuse. He took me into his remarkably cluttered house and unkempt kitchen, where he poured two small glasses of beautiful wine. We sipped it at a little table in his backyard, and talked about France. Over the weeks and months that led to our marriage two years later, I embraced this patient, kind, calm, and non-coercive man who had an insatiable curiosity and who stretched me intellectually. During that time he introduced me to his world, once bringing his obsolete but functional laboratory microscope to my kitchen, through which he helped me see penicillin growing on a piece of ginger root and yellow balls of ginger oil delicately held by a webbing of translucent cells. I was incapable of discussing most microbiological subjects, such as his research in "Plaques of Hemaglutination Inhibition by Individual Spleen Cells from Rabbits Immunized with

Influenza Viruses." However, our differences were minor and our shared interests multiple. Joe expressed his appreciation for our flourishing relationship with a gift that he created for me—a raku-fired bowl, embellished with green crackle glaze and inscribed *11 Jul 87* within.

We rediscovered legendary Brown County by spending our first Valentine's Day amid the rustic peace and early-twentieth-century ambiance of the Story Inn in the tiny town of Story. On August 25, 1989, family from across the country and Taiwan joined us there for our wedding dinner following our marriage in the Gothic-style, limestone-clad Beck Chapel on the campus of Indiana University in Bloomington. The morning following our wedding, after breakfast served on the inn's screened porch, many of us walked the country road beyond the inn, the cap on a sweet and joyful occasion. It was a landscape that drew us back over and over again.

The following May, on a twilight stroll near where we had set up camp in Brown County's Yellowwood State Forest, we were surprised and thrilled to see a whippoorwill and his mate on a branch above our heads silhouetted against the blue-black evening sky. Later, in the middle of the night, we were surprised again—when it began to rain. I stayed warm and dry in my sleeping bag while Joe crawled outside and dug a shallow trench around our tent to divert muddy rivulets. In the morning we hiked the Ten O'Clock Indian Treaty Line Trail, stopping along the way to squat down and photograph showy orchis, squawroot, and morel mushrooms. We also spotted a hawk guarding her nest in the top of a towering tree.

One portion of the trail follows a road that slopes through a forest and turns onto Duncan Road. At that corner, a classic back-country house with a sagging front porch and tin roof stood with a "For Sale" sign out front. Joe and I ambled by it, our minds whirling with the same unspoken thought. We slowed our pace, stopped, and turned around, and Joe put it into words: "Wouldn't it be great to have our own little place in Brown County?" We doubted that we could afford that little house, but we pursued the possibility. As it turned out, it was affordable, but the home inspector dashed that prospect when he advised that, should it become ours, we would be smart to tear it down and start over. Our realtor assured us that there were plenty of other places to buy in Brown County. The literature that he mailed us showed three possibilities, and we fell for the first one. In less than three months from that propitious May day, five acres, a "one-acre lake," and a three-room, six-hundred-square-foot, unstained board-and-batten cabin trimmed with barn-red paint became ours. That was where we would combine our creative energies and souls and where we expressed love in its broadest sense.

Because we were traveling that fall, our first overnight at the cabin was not until October 20. Since the furniture, mostly from Joe's house, wouldn't be delivered until a cold and rainy day in November, we spread sleeping pads and bags on the floor in camping fashion. Our table was a sheet of cardboard that spanned the space between a severed tree stump and a Styrofoam cooler. On that adrenaline-pumped first night, we were outside at 4:30 AM lying on our backs on the lawn, looking into a sky that was dark enough to identify constellations. Shooting stars whizzed by. Before breakfast we explored the "lake" region. Later, with the sun warming our backs, Joe read aloud from Charles Warren Stoddard's account of his ride in 1864 on muleback—up to, down, and across the crater of Mount Haleakala, Maui, where we had hiked three weeks earlier. Steeped in Stoddard's adventure, we were lured back into the wood's yellow, green, and orange panoply of fall foliage for one more walk before returning to the city.

The Lawsons, for whom our road was named in 1996, had owned a few hundred acres on both sides of the ridge, part of which they farmed. They donated a large portion to Camp Rancho Framasa and sold other sections to several buyers, including Annie Luebking, who bought around forty acres. When she became unable to live alone, near the end of the 1990s, she sold the last of her original purchase. But over a thirty-year period she had built a woodworking studio (which evolved into our cabin), her residence to the west of our cabin, and her next residence across the valley on what I affectionately call Annie's Ridge.

The woodworking studio had included a room for tables, lathes, and saws, a tiny bathroom, a small kitchen, and a garage. A recycler, Annie had installed pre-owned windows that varied in design. Some were metal-framed and slid sideways; some were wood-framed and multi-paned and opened with an iron crank; others, formerly storm windows, were held open by being propped inward on sturdy scavenged sticks. The three solid exterior wood doors had shims added to make them tight; one had a leaf cutout, Annie's touch. After Annie built her home with its own woodworking shop fifty feet away, she added a room on the forest side of the studio and turned the garage (a step down and sloping toward what had been the garage door) into a ten-by-twenty-foot bedroom. The former studio became a rental home.

Joe and I both enjoyed camping and being outdoors, but we reveled in the cabin's refinements—electricity, indoor plumbing, a solid roof, a phone, and heat. Even a refrigerator and stove came with the deal. At our new-to-us Brown County retreat, we were a step away from the outdoors we so loved but could be fully protected from adverse elements. We were so content with the cabin's comforts that months passed without our knowing the actual boundaries of our land. What do five acres look like on undulating topography, we wondered. Ben, our new neighbor, assured us that our land, contiguous with his, crossed the creek and extended up the opposite slope. We didn't believe that five acres could stretch that far until we located the corner stakes and acknowledged that Ben was correct. (In the spring of 1991, we purchased five additional acres from Annie.)

The cabin was good for all seasons, and we didn't imagine ever wanting more. Improvements began, nonetheless. I craved more light and better views, so a skylight went into the kitchen ceiling, windows were added at floor level on the forest side, and a glass-paneled door replaced a solid one. Joe couldn't tolerate the dirt and mud surrounding the cabin, so a deck replaced the unsteady wooden steps and bare ground at the back door, and creek gravel paths encircled the cabin. Retaining walls and solid steps made it safer to walk. Most of all, Joe abhorred the slippery mud slope strewn with rotting straw under the deck that led to the minuscule opening into the crawlspace and the water pump; so his "down under project" began. Crushed stone topped with creek gravel solved the problem created by the rivers of water that had eroded the drive during heavy rains. When "weeds" sprouted in the drive, I pulled them up, clearly an absurd use of my time. So we mowed the drive, sparing plants we thought were interesting. Now the drive is firm and even, green and mowed. The path to the dam and valley was once a log drag, an uninterrupted steep conduit for rainwater that gouged soil and ever-deeper troughs. Soil and water conservation agents advised us to embed slender tree trunks at intervals across the path at an angle to divert and slow the flow. Joe did that, then filled the troughs and planted annual rye. Moss and vegetation took hold again and ended the erosion.

My priorities were more form, Joe's more function. Occasionally my sense of aesthetics clashed with his functional acuity. He built a rack on the slope down from the cabin toward the pond. Wanting it to last a long time, he poured concrete into the spaces within some cement blocks, inserted square posts into the concrete, embedded the cement blocks in the ground, and spanned the distance between the posts with long boards on which he stored lumber and other odds and ends. It was practical, but in the winter it blocked a portion of our view of the pond from the cabin—a minor thing in the grand scheme, but a major one for me. I complained that it was an eyesore. He first tried appeasing me by stacking good firewood on the cabin side as a permanent camouflage of the storage space behind it. He hoped to make me happy and rescue his project as he made the "transformation." "Don't look," he said. My sweet husband didn't allow sores to fester, however, and soon afterwards he agreed that the camouflage hadn't worked and that the project was ill-conceived. As he dismantled it, he pledged to store the items elsewhere or simply throw them out.

During the first four years, overnight guests slept without complaint in the dismal bedroom, which was trimmed in dark wood and carpeted in soiled off-gold shag, while Joe and I slept on a marginally comfortable futon in the living room. It became clear that we needed two private sleeping rooms, so we had the single bedroom divided into two. Double walls were spaced three feet apart and bisected the long space crosswise, providing a closet for each room. The ceiling was raised to follow the roofline, and beams were added for strength. Where a closet once stood, two oak steps led through sliding glass doors to a gravel and stone patio. During those weeks of remodeling, we slept in the living room on top of the mattress and springs that were piled atop the futon. Plaster dust coated lamps, artifacts, books, carpet, and chairs. Brimming boxes and bags filled the floor space and most surfaces, with only the kitchen counter and the dining table kept clear to preserve my sanity.

Before the project was completed, I stood in the bedroom-to-be and looked out to the patio, where stepping stones curved across graveled space, branched at the garden wall, and led to the upper and lower paths. Indiana sandstone in shades of pink and apricot skirted the flower bed and colorfully accented the gray winter days. I stood outside and looked in. At night I switched on the interior bare bulbs to see how light from that evolving room would illuminate the patio. I was eager to awake to sunrise above our meadow. As a result of those improvements, Planet Venus's white light now pierces my closed eyelids in predawn hours and sunlight fills early mornings.

For more than six months, we worked to be ready for our first guests, whoever they might be. And yet, up to the moment when

Caroline and Tim Heine from Louisville turned into our drive on May Day, we were still scurrying around. Mini-blinds were mounted, a map of Indiana hung, a basement floor laid, a weather-tormented chest moved from its temporary resting place on the deck to storage, rusting buckets cleared from the back deck, the drain pipe jutting from behind the wood pile camouflaged, piles of lumber and green plastic pipes dispersed, and dead blossoms in the garden snipped. Craziness. But the improvements were appreciated by both our first and subsequent visitors. I extend my gratitude to the men who have made this cabin and the land livable and attractive— the craftsmen and carpenters, painters, handymen, excavators, plumber, landscaper, stonemason, tree trimmer, woodstove repairman, chimney sweep, and septic system monitor. Dave, Bill, Grover, Bob, Kenny, Jeff, Wyatt, Kevin, Mark, and Dan—all have graciously responded to provide more light and more views, safe drinking water from the tap, a room painted a happier color, and deer excluded from the gardens.

Joe developed a close sense of camaraderie with most of these men. Page, his brother, later wrote: "I recall from our earliest days that Joe always admired people who were skillful at what they did in whatever walk of life—washing windows, creating art with their hands, doing experiments, piloting airplanes, serving as forest and park rangers, or selling automobiles. He was always able to relate to what they were doing and drew them out about their work, thereby helping them to realize its significance. More often than not, he came to understand and appreciate the work so completely that he was able to give them direct help even though the field was new and unfamiliar to him."

Some of these men stayed too briefly—Mark Adams, for instance. A certified arborist, he was in Indiana tending our region's
trees while his wife earned her Ph.D. at Indiana University. We
hired Mark to trim limbs from several trees around the cabin. He
approached his work meticulously and respectfully. No "cherry
picker" for him; his climbing tools included ropes, pulleys, and a
trapeze or harness. With these he swung among the treetops like a
monkey as we stood below in awe and burst into applause when he
severed the final hefty oak branch, which he gently lowered to his
helper in the precise, predetermined location.

Grover Moore's ancestors settled in Brown County in the 1800s.
His foster family, however, moved from Ohio in the late 1930s when
work became available with the federal Works Projects Adminis-
tration (WPA) to build the Yellowwood State Forest dam. A handy-
man like his foster father, Grover also drives a Brown County school
bus, with kids ranging from kindergarten through twelfth grade.
He says that he has no problem keeping order on the bus. "Right
away I just try to be friends with 'em, and when I ask 'em to do
somethin', they do it." When he's not behind the wheel, he'll tackle
anything. Mow my small meadow in the early spring with his antique tractor? Stop the mudslide into the basement? Shore up the
sagging floor under the woodstove before it crashes into the crawlspace? Assemble storage cabinets? Plug up every possible mouse
entry into the utility closet? Change door locks? Move furniture
down from Indianapolis? His response is a quiet, modest "Sure, I
can do that."

Several young men assisted Joe with his "down under project"
beneath the front deck. This entailed converting the unprotected

earthen slope that led to the narrow entry into the crawlspace into a shop with fortress-like walls, a workbench, lights, running water, salvaged windows and screens, and a linoleum floor. In succession, Hobart, Matt (in training to play football for Brown County High School), and Wyatt, all strong teenagers, earned their wages with pick and shovel work, as Joe called it. The job required them to break up layers of sandstone (the pickax part), load it into a wheelbarrow (the shovel part), coast and brake the load down the hill (strong leg muscles required), dump it to divert runoff and fill gullies in the path to the meadow, then push the wheelbarrow back up to begin the next round. Joe mapped the course of action, and he also swung the pick, shoveled the stone, and used his strong legs to haul wheelbarrows loaded with debris down and push the empty containers back up. It was the kind of grueling but aerobic work that Joe, then in his seventies, liked for keeping fit. Wyatt worked closely with Joe, helping with his final projects—projects that his body ached to do, but ached painfully. Wyatt joined us for lunch one day and told us about his life and his Blackfeet Indian heritage. And there was the surprising moment when, shortly after arriving, he pulled off his knit cap and sheepishly revealed—green hair!

Two men were key to all—Dave Gore and Dan Gluesenkamp. Dave is a third-generation Brown Countian. His Grandpa Gore, a former school superintendent in Long Island, New York, read an article about Brown County in a 1949 issue of *Holiday* magazine. He came here, purchased 100 acres north of Nashville, and retired. Dave's folks, en route to Florida to build a motel, stopped to visit and didn't leave. They bought some acreage on State Road 135, lived temporarily in a little log cabin with a privy and no running water, and built their home and the Orchard Hill Motel. Dave is a respected craftsman who is also a musician. His voice and guitar playing can be heard on CDs such as *The Liar's Bench, My Brown County Home,* the two *A Brown County Home* Christmas albums, and *Lies and Love Songs.* The songs on *The Liar's Bench* reflect a touching and amusing confluence of Brown County history and tales. I guessed correctly that it is Dave who says on the CD, "It's a road so crooked it would break a snake's back."

Dave made all the improvements to the cabin. He is an aficionado of classical music, and with the radio tuned to WFIU, his hammer could be heard in synch with Vivaldi, Bach, and Mozart. He raised ceilings and built beams, added windows and a skylight, tore out a wall, built a wall, built a deck, replaced doors, and installed kitchen cabinets. The improvements were dramatic and exhilarating. But he never swerved from his intent to keep each alteration in harmony with the cabin's plain and simple form. Nothing fancy, yet every job met his high standards. Openings are straight and perfectly aligned. Screens close gently and with a soft click of the latches.

While I was away for a few days, Dave selected stones from the creek gravel paths and assembled them in tidy fashion on the aged timber that edges the walkway. They caught my attention when I came back, and then I got it: RUTH ANN, they spelled. Another time, while I was carrying stuff in from the car, I noticed a taupe-colored mushroom in my perennial garden with a cap about the size of a hamburger bun. For days this new species stayed firm. I had to photograph it before it decayed, so I got down on my knees with my camera and leaned over to peer under the cap at the gills and stem. It was not gilled, but rather a polypore—made of spray-painted Styrofoam. The stem? A pencil jammed into the ground. Dave's humor at work.

Dan and his Designscape crew did for the land what Dave did for the cabin. If it's manmade out there, it was done under Dan's watchful eye, as well as with his own muscle power, as he often joined his workmen. Joe and Dan worked closely and frequently side by side, swapping ideas and vision (and stories). They strove for an end result that was sturdy and solid and would last a long time. Dan recalled later: "Everything Joe said interested me. His talking was never futile. Although I didn't always agree, such as moving the rock from the basement down the hill to create a mini-dam, we were happy to do it, even though it was not cost-effective. Laughing all the way, the guys would go racing down the hill, letting the momentum carry the loaded wheelbarrow, fling it over, jump out of the way, and hike back up to do it over again."

One day I was pulling poison ivy vines in an area about twenty feet down the slope from the cabin when my gloved hand bumped into something hard. I brushed aside a layer of leaves and called to Joe: "I've found something made of metal." We removed layers of leaves, branches, and vines until the entire object was uncovered. It was a five-foot-wide square with numerous cutouts and the remains of a few rows of small wooden pins neatly inserted along one edge. In relief we read SCHOMACKER COLDSTRING PIANO MFG. CO. PAT'D APRIL 2, 1878 and SCHOMACKER CO PHILADELPHIA. We had uncovered the soundboard of an upright piano! A bit of detective work revealed the story. When Annie learned that a piano had been dropped at the dump, she asked a friend to pick it up and deliver it to her woodworking studio. She salvaged the ebony case and discarded the cast iron sounding board on the forest floor, where it had remained for a decade or so. Dan was here to plan the deer exclusion fence and noticed the sounding board leaning against a hickory tree where we had put it, not knowing what to do with such an artifact. Standing before it, he spread his arms wide and pronounced, "This will make a perfect gate." It was hauled away; heavy hinges were attached; and it was mounted to a deeply embedded post. It became our Pianogate.

Defining the lower patio is a curved wall built of massive hand-hewn blocks of stone, recovered from abandoned southern Indiana farm homes. The wall resembles the tapered tail of a giant scaly reptile. It was Joe's vision made real—a place to sit and converse or simply enjoy the view into the forest. Dan made it happen during Joe's final winter, his tribute to a friend.

Recently, Ken Patrick corrected some problems that developed after I had the dam reconstructed by an out-of-county firm. This gentle hulk of a man and his dozer worked as one entity—moving earth, lifting soft rock, scraping to hard rock, mixing clay slurry, rebuilding and packing clay, and evening out the fresh surface of the dam. Between the first and second repairs, we nearly lost him.

Ken told how he had broken through ice while fishing. He had left his eight-year-old grandson near the edge of a friend's frozen pond, where he had measured its thickness, and moved out nearer the center, fishing from a ladder stretched across the ice. After he had "pulled in" two bass, water started to flow over the ice. Soon Ken was in the water, and the ladder went down as he shouted to his grandson to go back. He tried hooking his foot above the ice to pull himself out, but had no luck. "At that time, I never thought about hollering," he said, adding that he was raised to believe that "if you got in a mess, you figured it out yourself." Nevertheless, he decided to yell a couple of times to see if anyone could hear him. Then, according to Ken, the miracle started to unfold. A man in a nearby house left the TV program he was watching to check a friend's car, which was leaking fluid. When he stepped outside, he heard the calls for help. He ran toward the pond, saw Ken, and shouted, "What can I do?" "Get a rope!" Ken yelled back. Luckily there was one nearby. He threw it to Ken and braced it on a pier as Ken hauled his three hundred pounds, plus his soaked outerwear, up and out. Ken then drove himself home. He called his rescuer that night. "I told him, 'If anything comes up and you need anything, you get ahold of me.'" In true Ken fashion he said, "I'd have done the same thing in his shoes, but I thank God he was there." The rescuer was quoted in the *Brown County Democrat:* "Mr. Patrick has something left to do in his life, and the Lord saw fit to use me for a neighbor in need."

With the expertise and goodwill of Hoosier folks like Grover, Dave, Dan, and Ken, changes continue here. With each change I send aloft the fervent wish that it be pleasing to Joe.

# An Essential Ingredient

A RELIABLE WATER SUPPLY has been a problem in Brown County. Water cannot penetrate the siltstone, shale, and sandstone beneath the soil's surface. Instead it runs off into streams that carve an "open drainage system." Consequently, with few exceptions, wells to tap groundwater are notoriously unsatisfactory here. Nineteenth-century pioneers settled near springs, when they could find them, or streams. Selma Steele writes in *The House of the Singing Winds* about the water situation in the first decade of the twentieth century: "Cisterns were not in use in our immediate locality. There were dug wells at the lower levels of the farms, also occasional springs. Both wells and springs were surface-fed, and dry during the dry periods of the year. Practically every hill farm had its puddle ponds, generally two of them: one for the stock and one for the household washing of clothes. Also there was the proverbial rain barrel which stood at the corner of the cabin." Kenny Patrick tells about a family with fourteen kids who lived down the road from his home when he was young. The family had a well, he said, but the water wasn't potable. So Ken and his brothers helped carry pails of water a quarter of a mile from a spring to the neighbor's cabin. Buckets of fresh water were lined up in the kitchen, he recalls.

New water towers have recently been erected, and water lines have been extended into more of the rural areas outside of Nashville, the county seat. Still, a large percentage of rural residents are not served. Alternative sources are pond and lake wells, truckloads of treated county water delivered and pumped into cisterns, and rainwater collected in cisterns from roof runoff. The latter is ideal for me, a part-time resident. An infrequent, unpredictable, and highly problematic alternative is unadulterated rain. It's lovely stuff on a hot and sultry summer day like one when I was drenched in sweat after mowing paths through the meadow. I finished the final swath and turned off the engine, then did something I had done only once before (in the predawn hours in my Indianapolis backyard). I dashed inside, stripped, grabbed soap, stood on the deck, and took a rain shower. Beware: If the rain stops while you're lathered in soap, it's important to have another available source of water. It did and I did.

"Why is it so hard to find people in Brown County to tell me about cisterns and cistern maintenance?" I asked Steve when he delivered water after I had had my cistern emptied and scrubbed clean. "It's a lost art—and besides, you see some disgusting things in cisterns." Grover came to help me solve a muddy problem caused by overflow from the cistern during heavy rains. With the cistern lid raised, he looked in and saw toads swimming in the water. He wondered why the lid had been resting on sticks, leaving a gap between the lid and the cistern collar. (To clean or repair a cistern, there must be an opening, or collar, large enough for a person to climb down in.) "To keep the lid from freezing shut," I explained, admittedly a lame excuse that midsummer day. Grover replied, "Frogs and snakes will get down in there. I used to find frogs and water snakes all the time when Mary Ann was here. She didn't watch it very close."

I ignore those remarks and collect rainwater in a 1,800-gallon concrete tank. With an average daily water usage of 20 gallons (compared to the average American's usage of 100 gallons), my annual consumption would be 7,300 gallons (four tanks full) if I lived here 365 days a year. Using the formula in the *Cottage Water Systems* book, which states that twelve inches of rain yields 5 gallons of water per square foot of roof (flat measurement, not pitched), I would collect twice as much as needed, based upon an average annual rainfall of forty inches. In more than ten years of measuring and recording the cistern level (as well as the rainfall and pond levels), the amount in the cistern has not fallen below 1,400 gallons, other than when it was deliberately drained. Typically the tank has 1,650 gallons or more when I arrive, enough to meet my needs for three months without an additional drop of rain. Larger-capacity cisterns should make it possible for a small family to manage on collected water.

For the first year, we drew water directly from the cistern to the tap and used it for everything, including drinking. Rainwater flowed from the roof into gutters and downspouts, then passed through catchments containing a mix of activated charcoal and gravel, and into the cistern. The family that had lived here previously used the system as we found it, we were told, and a local friend said he grew up on cistern water and never had a problem. However, from time to time Joe and I experienced minor GI tract problems that we didn't, at first, relate to our drinking water. But nagging questions remained: What about animal droppings on the roof? Were our catchments really removing contaminants? Unsure, we began to bring water in five-gallon containers to be used for drinking and cooking.

By 1998, the tap water had begun to smell foul. My showers became counterproductive. I drew a water sample using the kit supplied by the Indiana State Board of Health. The test results confirmed my fear that harmful bacteria were present. Remembering Steve's words about nasty things in cisterns, I searched the yellow pages for local water treatment specialists. Finding none, I selected a firm in Boone County (northwest of Indianapolis) that was recommended by a friend. Although short on experience with cisterns, they devised a system, and two workmen drove down to finalize the plans, offering free labor in exchange for permission to hunt wild turkey on my property. A deal.

I had the cistern emptied and sprayed with chlorine. The turkey hunters shoveled out the useless, foul charcoal and gravel in the catchments, added new, and installed a tank with activated charcoal to remove the chlorine that I poured periodically (and unscientifically) into the cistern. The tank was refilled with county water and supersaturated with more chlorine. This was drawn into the pipes and allowed to remain there awhile to kill any bacteria. Subsequently, I monitored the resulting concentration in the cistern with a chlorine test kit, the kind used for swimming pools, and drank the water with confidence. But by summer's end the hot water again had a foul odor. Local plumber Bill Dunham, who was intimately familiar with Brown County water systems, agreed to help. He drained the hot water tank and filled it with chlorinated water, thereby solving that problem. Safe again, I thought, except for my persistent concern about the many variables and the still-imprecise approach to bacteria-free water. Indeed, two years later, another test revealed more undesirable bacteria in a water sample drawn from the tub's faucet.

Bill conferred with a water treatment engineer in Chicago, who suggested an automated system. Now, with each pull of the pump, water is drawn from the cistern into an airtight holding tank, and chlorine is simultaneously injected into the same tank. Upon need, chlorinated water is pulled through activated charcoal to remove the chlorine and enters the pipes. My tap water is safe and excellent to drink.

Some say that there are more manmade lakes and ponds in Brown County than in Indiana's other ninety-one counties combined. Most were created after the mid-twentieth century to supply water. Water may be drawn directly from the pond or lake or from a well dug at the shoreline. These bodies of water, which dot the county, also provide recreation. In addition, they can be used for fire control

with the installation near roads of "dry fire hydrants," non-pres-
surized pipe systems that make it possible for firefighters to obtain
water without having to drive a long distance.

Our pond, twelve to fourteen feet at its deepest point when full,
was created when the cabin was constructed in the early 1970s. Perhaps it was intended to be a water source, but I'm unaware that it
was used in that way. Two ravines, which form the pond's water-
shed, converge and create its distinctive boomerang shape. Oak trees
that grow on the surrounding slopes leach tannin into the soil and
give the pond water its characteristic tea color. Originally, red maple,
sycamore, and multiple tulip poplar trees were allowed to grow on
the dam, which lent the area a natural look. A "J"-shaped, white
corrugated pipe slanted through the dam and jutted out the back
side in order to maintain the desired water level. A spillway, eighteen inches higher than the outlet, carried water away rapidly during heavy rains and prevented it from eroding the broad lip of the
dam. Water coursed along the spillway and poured over the slope,
where the white torrent divided into a network of streamlets tumbling over one another to merge with Cassie Creek.

Curious to know where the pond's overflow ends up, I once
traced its route on local and state maps. Cassie Creek joins the
stream, which purls along beside Wallow Hollow and Clay Lick
Roads; it then joins North Fork Salt Creek, which later spreads
out into what is now Monroe Reservoir; it passes around the dam
and eventually merges with the East Fork of White River, which
meets the West Fork, becoming White River, and thence onward to
the Wabash, the Ohio, the Mississippi, and finally the Gulf of
Mexico.

The first time Joe and I stood at the edge of our "one-acre lake" (the claim on the realtor's promotional piece), we instantly dismissed it as anything of value. The black-brown color and steep bare dirt slopes made it look like a tar pit that sultry July afternoon. We assumed, incorrectly, that it was biologically dead. We thought that the summer foliage blocking our view of the disgusting pond from the cabin was an advantage. A year later, our understanding of it had reversed, and we looked forward to autumn, when the pond would reappear. Then we could see coppery sunsets reflected on its surface, erratic agitation from fish leaping to snatch delicate insects drifting above the water, and broadly spaced concentric circles from wood ducks stopping by to lounge, feed, and frolic. Our *one-third-acre pond* is a treasure—a lure for wildlife, a grand skating rink in winter, and a refreshing swimming hole in summer.

Late in May our first spring here, I plunged into an aquatic space shared by tadpoles sprouting legs, whirligig beetles, a painted turtle, hundreds of fish, and unknown numbers of tinier inhabitants. Heavy rains had filled the pond; the air and water temperatures were ideal; the water was clear. There were no concrete walls to bump into and no chlorine or sea salt to sting my eyes. Joe did not enjoy swimming, but an inflatable boat made it possible for him to be on the water while I swam. At times we paddled together from one shore to another and giggled, delighted that we had inadvertently acquired a bonus, our pond.

By midsummer the water level had dropped significantly, and despite the heat and humidity, I resisted taking cooling swims. Instead I read a book by Joyce Carol Oates while floating in the little boat and reveled in my ultimate getaway. I began to see schools of bass and several catfish languidly swimming in the shallows, including one that appeared to be eighteen inches long with a five-inch-wide head and three-inch whiskers.

I've learned to ignore less-than-optimum conditions. If the pond is covered with an oily film, caused by decaying vegetative matter, I happily stroke my way around, leaving a trail of brown bubbles behind. On an oppressively hot day in 1995, when Christy was back for a visit, she followed me into the pond, despite her reservations about the sheen. Sweet relief. Then two biting flies dashed for our wet heads. Determined to drive us out of their territory, they dove at us repeatedly. We gulped air and submerged; we beat the surface and yelled; we spun and made menacing walls of water with our hands. Ultimately, the small but mighty flies were victorious.

Now when I swim, I am usually alone, with no one around. In June 2002, my first husband, the father of my two daughters, drowned accidentally while following the route of Meriwether Lewis's canoe trip in the early 1800s down the Ohio River from Pittsburgh. I do think about his drowning when I'm alone in the middle of the pond, and I do consider the impact my drowning would have on my family, but I haven't given up the pleasure.

If algal blooms form in hot, dry weather, the water resembles thin soup. At those times, the pond may also emit a putrid aroma. A combined treatment of blue dye and bacteria works to correct both problems. The dye works by deflecting the sun's rays from the algae, thus slowing its growth; the bacteria work by eating the algae as well as the oily film. An aeration system is a future possibility.

When the pond freezes, it becomes my ice rink. One winter

day, with newly sharpened blades on my skates, I whirled and circled and did "three turns." There was none of the waltz music amplified over a loudspeaker that I was accustomed to when skating at the Indiana State Fair coliseum. The hazard here was not from colliding with other skaters but from tangling with overhanging tree branches. Overhead, clouds like gigantic cotton balls floated across a cerulean sky. Tips of tree branches, encrusted with ice diamonds, sparkled in the sun. Bluebirds feasted on sumac berries.

Once, to determine the safety of the ice, Joe bored holes with a hand drill to measure the thickness, beginning near the edge and moving inward. "Seven inches in the center," he declared. So on another cold afternoon, I skated fearlessly over a surface rough from snow that had fallen on ice, then been rained upon and frozen again. I rumbled across a crack, which had opened and refrozen, and a ridge or two, before practicing more "three turns" on isolated patches of smooth ice.

One spring, Joe and I slept beside our beloved pond in sleeping bags. That bright moonlit night, a whippoorwill, a great horned owl, and spring peepers serenaded us to sleep, and a Louisiana waterthrush awakened us in the morning. Before my eyes were fully open, Joe hiked up to the cabin, prepared coffee, and returned to serve me my morning caffeine "in bed."

In midwinter, the pond was usually full. But each summer the level dropped three, four, and sometimes five feet below the outlet. That pattern worsened over the years. Trees that grew in the dam were part of the problem. The drainage pipe had become corroded or had a broken seal, and water was entering it several inches below its intake. Water was even leaking under the dam's base, I was later told. I had that old dam deconstructed and a new one built. Sadly, the new dam was not "keyed" properly to tight, solid rock. Water leaked through the disturbed layers of soft rock underlying the spillway, and later, water broke through the mid portion of the dam. Ken Patrick did the corrective work.

The pond is a thriving wildlife habitat. It is home to a variety of fish, snapping and painted turtles, whirligig beetles and water striders, numerous frog species, and dragonflies and damselflies; a stopping place for wood ducks, mallards, other birds, and mammals; and a place for bats to snatch insects in the air and scoop drinks of pond water as they swoop by. Once dismissed as biologically comatose, the pond now lures numerous species—including mine.

*Upper left:* I was happy that this widow skimmer dragonfly took a break from hunting prey so that I could take its photograph.

*Upper right:* This sleek cone-headed grasshopper had a great view of the world from its golden platform atop a black-eyed Susan in the meadow.

*Right:* Soon after Joe and I purchased our "hideaway," we decided to allow the lawn to become a naturalized garden. Now it sparkles with plant diversity and teems with life.

I find that of all the seeds I offer my avian friends, sunflower seeds are liked by most birds, including this male cardinal cracking its way through a pile on my rail.

This American toad called my bluff when I got down with it eye to eye.

Airy serviceberry trees bloom slightly ahead of the better-known dogwoods.
Here a serviceberry embellishes my spring view of the valley meadow.

A favorite moment in my winter day occurs when the rising sun anoints
Annie's Ridge, as seen here from my cabin.

I am continuously delighted by nature's myriad forms, including this jelly-type fungus of the *Tremella* family oozing from a long-dead branch.

Among the first fungi I photographed were these shelf-like turkey tails growing on a log in a decaying woodpile.

*Left:* I love the way this fragile *Russula* seems to illuminate its dark surroundings.

*Bottom:* If I were giving this fungus a common name, it would be bean sprouts. Others call it fairy fingers or white worm coral.

These exquisite and uncommon pink Indian-pipes have appeared only once in my more than a dozen years here. I was able to photograph them from the time they broke through the earth until they matured and turned black weeks later.

I did not know of the existence of the common marsh pink until after Joe and I purchased our Brown County cabin. It is now my favorite native flower.

Saint Andrew's-Cross is an unusual native flower that is easily overlooked.
I see it only infrequently.

Now that I have a small meadow in place of a lawn, birds and insects, such as this great spangled fritillary, can find plenty of nourishment.

I was fortunate to have spotted this goldenrod spider with its bumblebee prey. Later, in the subsequent photograph, I noticed the inchworm keeping a comfortable distance.

This eastern tiger swallowtail was probing for nectar in the flower of a blackberry lily, a plant that I started from seeds collected while on a late summer walk.

Scarlet waxy caps glow in the warm rays of the afternoon sun. In 1997, this photo won first place in the 13th Annual Limberlost Nature Photography Contest.

*Top:* Of the dozens of mushrooms that I've photographed, this *Bulgaria rufa* is one of the most handsome. It grows on buried sticks under leaf mold or soil.

*Bottom:* Year after year I see these velvety members of the Lactarius family growing at the base of a ravine in gravelly soil. When cut across the gills, they exude a milky sap.

I rarely see the more striking caterpillars such as this io moth larva. You need to be careful with this one, as contact with its spines causes stinging pain.

In the spring I see elegant eastern snipe flies like these mating on a forsythia leaf. It took several years and finally an e-mailed query to a University of Illinois entomologist before I was able to learn their true identity.

This thread-waisted wasp was floundering in my birdbath when I scooped it to the safety of an outdoor tablecloth. It spent a long time drying its various parts— wings, legs, and antennae.

I snapped this picture of a net-winged beetle a few moments before it flew
from a sprig of ironweed that was resting on my railing.

*Left:* When I first noticed this destroying angel next to my path, I gasped at its pristine beauty. I hiked up to the cabin to retrieve my camera and then went back down again. Incidentally, this alluring *Amanita* is fatal if eaten.

*Bottom:* I find that winter's beauty sometimes takes subtle forms, as in this natural assemblage of lichen, moss, acorn, and oak leaves.

*Right:* In the winter, I enjoy a mug of steaming tea made from the roots of indigenous sassafras trees. In late summer, birds feast on the sassafras fruit, happily devouring these deep-blue delicacies.

*Bottom:* Some tree leaves are as colorful in their infancy as they are in maturity. I particularly like these tiny oak leaves that look as though they were dipped in red raspberry juice.

Brown County is a scenic destination in October when the leaves turn brilliant colors, as on these branches arching overhead near my cabin.

# Cold and Hot

SHADES OF BROWN replace the recent colorful spectrum. Stems of spent plants jut from mats formed from dark, soggy layers of withered leaves. Tree branches compose a chaotic, three-dimensional network. Precipitation falls as cold rain, sleet, ice, and snow. Friends and family visit, and I cook pancakes to golden perfection on the woodstove. Later we drink hot buttered rum and read poetry aloud while nourishing soup simmers. Candlelight illumines our dinner.

One cold night I read *Solar Storms* by Linda Hogan and contrasted my cozy winter scenes to life for Native Americans near the boundary waters of Minnesota, not far from Grand Rapids, where Joe was born. Hogan, a Chickasaw poet, novelist, and essayist, writes:

The houses themselves were small, some patched with tarpaper, pieces of metal, packing crates, or whatever else had been available. They had originally been built by missionaries some years ago and put together for the sole purpose of warmth. Inside them, in the long, deep winters, men went silent for months while lonely women, surrounded by ice and glacial winds, stood at windows staring out at the vast white and frozen world, watching for signs of spring: a single bud, a stem of green, as if spring were a lover come to rescue them from winter's bleak captivity.

In my winter world, books, newspapers, the Internet, radio, television, and phone shield me from debilitating isolation; my cabin protects me from winter's inclemency; my woodstove warms me.

To stay warm means planning ahead and handling wood. When I hoist and toss split wood into a wheelbarrow from the mound dumped at the top of the drive, push it across the mole bumps to the wood rack, lift it again, and stack it, I wonder if friends outside of Brown County have a clue about life here. In contrast to my urbane demeanor, there is this other with wash-and-wear hair, stained jeans, torn gloves, and flushed, sweating face as I labor to be somewhat self-reliant and prepare for winter. The fact is that if you use a wood-burning stove for heat, you handle wood—a lot of it— and that requires physical effort.

To the best of my knowledge, gas furnaces have kept me warm most of my life. In Indianapolis I align the temperature on the thermostat with my comfort zone, and the old behemoth in the basement fires up and blows hot air through the ducts and out the registers. It's effortless, magical, different from the primary heating system for the cabin—a practical but demanding wood-burning stove. The stove may be magical in its own way, but it's not effortless. Nevertheless, despite the work involved in heating with wood, I rarely turn to the costly electric heat emitted from base heaters.

Before our second winter here, the old, inefficient stove that had come with the cabin was gone, replaced by a modern Vermont Casting Defiant cast iron stove. It has a dull black finish, glass-paned doors, and a catalytic converter to reduce air pollutants. For good fire gazing it is elevated seven inches from the floor on a platform faced with ceramic tiles. That's that, you say—there's the stove; add wood; end of subject. Not so. You have to locate a source for split wood, store it covered for a year to season it, build the fires, and maintain the stove. And there are the aesthetics, the magic.

Most of the wood I burn is purchased from excavators. Odd, isn't it, since the cabin snuggles up to a mixed hardwood forest? But the main portion of my forest is on steeply sloped terrain below the cabin. Pushing anything uphill, including chunks of wood in a wheelbarrow, is work for the strong. Better to buy a cord or two of split firewood, have it dumped in the drive above the cabin, and let gravity and a wheelbarrow do most of the work.

In the midst of the heating season, I both wonder if what I have stacked around will get me through the current winter and think about finding a supply of good wood for the next one. For $35 to $55, I can purchase a rick of wood of variable quality. (A rick is a pile of wood eight feet long, four feet high, and the depth of one stick, or eighteen inches in my case.) A higher price does not guarantee better wood. Joe was fussy about firewood. He grumbled over twisted, oddly shaped pieces with branch stubs jutting out, and I agree with him. Such pieces are hard to stack and fit awkwardly in the stove. Invariably there are uneven pieces, so I stash them on top of the wood pile and burn them first to get them out of the way.

One of our first firewood deliveries included sticks of Osage orange. This wood, the heart of which is colored deep orange, has historic significance in the United States and is thoroughly described in *PrairyErth* by William Least Heat-Moon. It burns hot, so I save it for extremely cold weather. Beware, though: when jostled, it explodes like fireworks into a spray of bright orange pinhead-sized fragments, and when the stove doors are opened for loading more wood, it will burn holes in clothing and flooring. There are other good-burning woods, and bad ones, too. I place oak in the *excellent* category. Oak is a dense wood that grows abundantly in Brown County and burns hot and long. Hickory, favored by many, also burns well, but it leaves deep piles of ash residue on the stove grid, which I dislike. After a year burning logs from a tulip poplar tree that was cut to make way for my reconstructed dam, I put it into my *barely tolerable* category, as it does not burn hot and burns too quickly. Pine, in the form of scrap lumber (few coniferous trees grow in Brown County region), is not advised because of the fire hazard from the creosote it deposits on chimney walls.

Joe was a systematist, in a narrow sense a pyromaniac, and the fire's keeper. Actually a pro, he had studied the properties of fire and co-authored a patent on "proteinaceous fire-fighting foaming agents." Against the wall behind the stove he built a multi-compartment storage rack from three-quarter-inch plywood to hold supplies and varying sizes of wood, from the smallest kindling to the thickest, heaviest pieces. He taught me to build good fires and gave me the confidence to take over when I became the fire's sole keeper. But once on my own, I simplified the system. I had the storage unit dismantled, and I now keep a ready supply of wood stacked outside, near the back door for easy access. Unfortunately, Joe did not teach me how to split wood for kindling (I may be unteachable), so I cut fallen branches into small pieces with a chainsaw and use them instead.

A major helper came in the form of a gift from my neighbor June, who contributed a product called Hot Flashes for my early lone fire-building efforts. "Use *Firestarters for Women*," according to the wrapper, "and you don't need a man . . . to light your fire!" The idea originated with a Virginia woman who "discovered, after losing her dear husband, that she had never learned to make a good Manhattan nor to light a fire in the fireplace." They "help women blaze their way across gender and generation gaps." Made from a combination of melted candle wax and sawdust, they've helped me get hundreds of fires going. For each package of Hot Flashes sold, a donation is made to the National Breast Cancer Coalition.

Stove maintenance is a minor expense of major importance. A good chimney sweep is crucial, though it seems to be a dying profession. A sweep cleans the stove parts and the stack to prevent chimney fires. However, after a sweep performed the annual maintenance in 2000, I had a frightening experience. I confidently lit my first fire that fall season. Half an hour later, I laid two logs atop a shallow bed of red coals, and they took off, as they should. The stove thermometer soared past my preferred 500–600 degree temperature range, shot up to 750 degrees, and kept climbing, even though the handle that controls the primary air shutter was in the closed position. When I discovered that the handle wasn't working

and the shutter was stuck fully open, a sick feeling of panic en-
gulfed me. Alice Vollmar, my houseguest from Minnesota, was show-
ering and was unaware of the drama—and in no position to help
me. I had to get at least one log out to slow the fire, so I opened the
stove doors and used long-handled tongs to grab a blazing log. I
carried it across the room and out to the back deck, where I had
first placed a metal roasting pan. The pan, though shorter than the
flaming piece of wood, kept the log off the flammable wood deck.
With a strong wind blowing that night, I was appropriately fearful
that it would loft a spark from the burning log and start a fire in
the tinder-dry leaf bed inches away. Since I had left the doors to
the stove wide open and its red-hot contents unshielded, I rushed
back in, closed the doors, rushed back out, and began pouring buckets of water over the log until it stopped steaming. All's well. . . .

❧

The even warmth from the woodstove is unlike the on-again,
off-again heat from a forced-air furnace. One dark, frigid December evening it was 38 degrees inside when Joe and I arrived. We got
the fire going and pulled our chairs near the stove, our knees nearly
touching its glass doors. I shivered inside my down jacket as we ate
Brie with French bread and crackers accompanied by bourbon on
ice, followed by a dessert of apples with bran crunch cookies accompanied by port wine. Inch by inch we moved back as the cabin,
and we, warmed up.

The wood-burning stove is more than a source of quiet, even,
comforting, friendly warmth. It's also my cookstove—fine for
braised chicken, steamed vegetables, homemade soups, toasted

bread, puddings, and pancakes. I treasure the concept of using one energy source to heat the cabin and cook meals. And when I place a slice of stone-ground whole wheat bread on the stovetop to toast, I chuckle with delight.

Then there are those times when, surrounded by silence and darkness, I crouch before the stove and watch a flame—one steady, unbroken orange ribbon. Slightly nearer, a U-shaped rainbow-colored flame floats up from its source, wavers, and settles back down, doing a slow dance over and over. Beneath it all, a quivering, fiercely hot orange bed of coals fuels the fire. Volcanic.

It is winter and the leaves have fallen, baring skeletal trees. The clear nights are prime for looking into outer space. My tall bedroom window frames a northerly view where the handle of the Big Dipper, like a diamond-studded chain, laces its way through the trees and touches the curve of the near ridge; where, on February 25, 1997, comet Hale-Bopp's plume, 123 million miles near, marked the blackness like a broad stroke of chalk; and where one meteor, then another and another flashed past in the early morning of December 13, 1998. Dozens more followed until dawn's light finally masked the Geminid meteor fragments that, unseen, continued sizzling in Earth's upper atmosphere.

Somewhat removed from the "sickly orange glow" of urban light pollution that robs us of the pleasure of nighttime's celestial treats, Brown County has relatively dark nights. David H. Levy, discoverer of twenty-one comets, is a founder of the International Dark-Sky Association, a pragmatic coalition of astronomers and lighting industry interests. Its mission is to preserve and protect our heritage of dark skies through outdoor lighting that does not spill upward. As one advocate put it, "I want to see stars, not light bulbs." Many cities (including Los Angeles) and states, and even one country, the Czech Republic, have recently passed light-control measures. Thankfully, in Brown County when I step outside on moonless, cloudless winter nights, I can see glittering star dots prick the skyscape, the Great Nebula in Orion's sword glow softly amid numberless numbers of stars, and the filmy galactic spectacle, our Milky Way, arch from horizon to horizon. Looking up and out, I think about Scott Russell Sanders's *Writing from the Center:*

> The more geographers reveal about the earth and the more astronomers reveal about the universe, the harder it is for us to believe in the cosmic importance of any spot. Viewed from the moon, the grandest metropolis is only a molehill. The earth itself is no more than a speck of grit in a run-of-the-mill galaxy. And our entire galaxy, viewed from a few light years away, dwindles to the size of a struck match.

Millions remember the Leonid meteor shower on November 18, 2001, when Earth passed, head-on, through streams of debris from Periodic Comet Tempel-Tuttle. June, my neighbor, and I agreed to meet in her drive at 4:30 AM. The night before, I laid ready-to-grab layers of clothing next to the bed and slept in long underwear so that I would feel toasty when I threw aside the covers in the early hours and could rapidly pile on plenty of clothes. Multiple layers weren't needed, however, since the temperature was in the upper forties and the air was calm. June was already out and had seen a few streaks. In spite of light fog, we saw the show, including those that flashed near our horizon. After June left, I pulled a chair to my upper drive, where I stayed until 6:30. Dozens upon dozens of meteoroids, generally ranging from the size of large sand grains to small pebbles in a 22,000-mile-thick band that orbits the sun, streaked and flashed as they vaporized in Earth's upper atmosphere at altitudes of about forty to eighty miles. Some exploded and lit the darkness like a camera's flash in a dark room. The tails of some vanished the instant they appeared, while others made white paths that briefly spanned more than half the sky. Three cloudy plumes, which I watched with binoculars, remained visible ten minutes and more, changing from straight lines to curved then jagged ones. Were they buffeted by upper stratospheric winds? By midmorning I knew that June and I had been fortunate, as friends and relatives in Indianapolis, Virginia, and Montana e-mailed to report that clouds and fog had ruined their celestial shows.

What, in addition to good skygazing, defines winter in south-central Indiana? The month of December? Perhaps. But consider this string of days in the twelfth month of 1996: Friday—snow-covered; Saturday—65 degrees in the sun; Sunday—snowy and sub-freezing; Monday—sunny and chilly; Tuesday—cloudy and warm; Wednesday—60 degrees at 5:30 AM. Well, then, January? In mid-January 1994 it was minus 30 degrees; in mid-January one year later, it was 64 degrees—a 94 degree difference.

Perhaps the following scenarios best describe winter here. One January day in 1992, I cross-country skied while Joe squeezed into the crawlspace to focus a lamp on the frozen sewer line and plug in an electric heater. That night our footprints traced the outline of moon shadows cast by surrounding trees onto the snow-covered valley floor. Since the water lines were also frozen, we hauled buckets of water up from the cistern, warmed it on the stove, and plunged it into the toilet to restore the flow. That's a wintertime dilemma. This scene, too, defines winter here: One year ice rained and enveloped every blade of grass, twig and branch, seed and berry cluster until the temperature inched above freezing, and the melting ice made the chattering noise of a gentle rainfall splattering on the leaf-covered earth. Once-tall prairie grasses, bent and burdened by glassy shrouds, creaked and groaned, slowly collapsing as their ice supports melted. Strong winds that night broke loose the remaining fragments of ice.

More than once in the early years, we failed to make it up the final snow-covered hill in Joe's sedate gray Ford Escort station wagon. After several futile attempts, with nerves frayed and spinning tires spewing the noxious scent of burned rubber, we would quit, back down, and abandon our car along the roadside. Ben, our neighbor, would come to the rescue in his trusty, rusty pickup truck, ferrying our gear and us, along with Cassie, to the cabin. Obviously the Ford was inadequate, so Joe bought a used cherry-red four-wheel-drive Jeep Cherokee. After the new vehicle's first successful test, when it forged up the steep incline without hesitation, cut a track through snow ten inches deep, and coasted down the drive to our steps, Joe took a picture of me standing next to the Jeep with my arms raised in a sign of victory.

Unfortunately, a different challenge awaited. The temperature was minus 27 degrees. "It's cold enough to freeze your butt off" came to mind when we discovered our only toilet bowl filled with a block of ice, requiring us to make alternative arrangements. An icicle hung from the kitchen faucet, and bottled water was frozen solid in the refrigerator. We had been caught off guard and unprepared for the severely cold weather. With all five electric base heaters turned fully on and a fire roaring in the woodstove, the pipes eventually thawed. The next day, however, the water line between the cistern and the pump failed, and snowmelt became our water source again. Throughout it all, Joe was euphoric. Wearing a down coat, a facemask, thick gloves, heavy socks, and boots, he headed outside and declared, "This is great! This is how I remember Minnesota winters!"

I too love winter and yearn for snow. Curvy and usually soft, it embellishes, conceals, and, conversely, reveals, as in the valley meadow, where bird tracks crisscross under seed-bearing grasses and flowers. Once I saw a set of tracks that vanished in mid-path, next to a snow-embossed fan of wings: "a rabbit or mouse lifted up in the claws of a hungry god," in Linda Hogan's words.

The world was a frozen one. Walking was noisy. Leaves were flat, frozen masses glued together by ice that snapped crisply underfoot. Where a thin surface layer of earth had been pushed up, supported by tiny brittle columns of ice, the sound was hollow. Ice pendulums shaped like elongated teardrops formed on branches hanging slightly above the rapidly flowing creek; foam had been transformed into frozen white pillows. Frozen puddles brought back memories of long-ago walks to grade school when I was fortunate to be the first to come upon street puddles freshly glazed with ice. I replayed the sound of the ice stretching and then popping when I pushed against thin ice with the toe of my boot.

That morning I had read *Photography and the Art of Seeing* by Freeman Patterson. It was as though the author were there to physically place the camera and tripod in my hands and shove me out the

door. Down to the valley I went and captured ephemeral ice forms
on film.

Two inches of wet snow had fallen. When I turned on the back
light to admire the snow-covered evergreens one more time before
going to bed, a small, football-shaped light-tan ball of feathers
caught my eye. Perched near the far upper edge of the screen door,
which was propped open as usual to make transporting firewood
easier, was a screech owl watching for prey. Perhaps it anticipated
little mice scurrying to the tray of seed I had been leaving for the
birds. I admired it from different angles for several minutes, then
shut the inner door and turned off the light, leaving the bird to its
silent quest.

New Year's Day 1999, I awoke to snow-covered vistas. The temperature was zero. Despite the weather, Zach and Fran Brahmi came
down from Indianapolis for a midday meal and scooted back with
little time to spare as a warm upper layer of air flowed over a cold
one and ice fell on top of the snow, followed by more snow. The
scene was stunning, but walking through it was difficult. With each
step, the surface supported my weight momentarily before I broke
through. To take a next step, I had to lift my foot up and out of the
hole. Birds fed ravenously, and a junco and a Carolina wren squeezed
through an inch-wide entry into the protected storage space under
the deck. Christy breezed in slightly ahead of the storm, stopping
first for essentials at the local IGA, where the bread shelves were
empty, milk was down to pint containers, and only half-dozen car-
tons of eggs remained. We hunkered down that night and felt deli-
ciously protected inside the cabin.

February. It may start out frosty, but inevitably days will climb into the sixties. Although the environment appears to be in deep slumber, a close look will reveal signs of spring. Peel back the outer layer of forsythia buds to see bright green leaves tightly pressed together, ready and waiting. Daylight hours increase and sunshine rejuvenates. Tree sap flows. Cardinals, chickadees, titmice, and song sparrows jubilantly cheer spring's approach. Sandhill cranes pass on their way back from Georgia and Florida to their northern breeding grounds.

March. On a warm day in this transitional month, Joe swung in the hammock until my parents arrived from Indianapolis. We sipped chilled fruit drinks outside while my father repeated stories about his flying days in the 1920s. Shorts and short-sleeved shirts were suitable attire for a walk in the woods, where distinctive green leaves of clover, daisy, daffodil, wintercress, and toothwort cheered us. A pileated woodpecker filled the valley with a reverberating, territorial tattoo. But a mere three days later, snow blanketed the ground and the air was a windy 33 degrees. Nuthatches, pushy and aggressive, hunched their shoulders, fanned their tails, opened their beaks, and lurched toward other birds that attempted to share their feeder space. Another feeding station had two dozen birds at once. Did they sense what meteorologists predicted, another six to eight inches of snow to come before the final thaw?

# Mousy

"Mousy": "Lacking in boldness, colorless, timid," according to my dictionary. This does not describe the mice that called my Brown County cabin home for ten years.

Fortunately, I am not afraid of mice. However, under normal circumstances, those that find their way into my Indianapolis home are eliminated with snap traps. There was a time, though, when I uncovered a nest of baby mice while turning my compost pile. Concurrently, I disturbed a colony of ants, which instantly crawled into every orifice of the helpless little creatures. I plucked the babies from the dirt, brushed the ants off of them, put them in a box, took them to the breakfast room, and fed them for days—until some climbed out. They were home free, untouched by our cat, Miss Chat, who didn't conceive of herself as a predator of mice. Those left behind in the box went to my daughter Lisa's grade-school class for nature study.

Joe and I committed to live with nature when we came to Brown County. We were the interlopers. Mice changed our minds.

I believe that most of the mice that fed, bred, and played in the cabin were white-footed mice, *Peromyscus leucopus,* and not their close relative deer mice, *P. maniculatus.* They are beautiful rodents with prominent, bulging eyes, large rounded ears, and fur the color of golden oak, with white feet and bellies. Their bodies are three to four inches long, and their bicolored tails are two and a half to four inches long, with tufts of fur at the end. They are nocturnal.

The first one we saw hopped back and forth past Christy, who was stretched out on the floor for a short nap. How could the poor little creature survive? To help it, we opened a can of peanuts and watched it devour a few. Another time, one ran back and forth within inches of my toes while I stood near the kitchen cabinets talking on the phone. Tiny gray things obligingly curled into a ball as the mother mouse carried each into the abyss behind the kitchen cabinets. We were still in the aren't-they-cute phase!

Busy, determined creatures, they entered through hidden openings for years. No place seemed out of reach; their droppings testified to that. Thoughts of extermination came out in our conversations until a naturalist friend described the awful death that results from some methods—desiccation from common mouse poison and equally slow death from sticky tape that holds their feet and doesn't let go. Exclusion is the humane method, he urged. We nodded in agreement. We admired their adaptability, their fleetness, and their survival skills, and because of their endearing appearance, our initial approach was to live-trap and release them. We finally blocked access to the kitchen drawers, and I no longer had to wash all the flatware each time we came.

They tucked chunks of Cassie's dry dog food under my bed pillow and stored salted and buttered toasted almonds, negligently left overnight on the counter, in my hiking boot. We increased our assault and set both spring and Hav-A-Hart traps. We carried the live-trapped mice further and further away; one we took to the other side of Cassie Creek. The flowing stream would be a barrier, like a moat, we assumed. The mouse jumped from the opened trap, dashed in the direction of the cabin, ran/swam across the creek in three seconds, scampered up the bank, and disappeared in leaf litter. At that rate, it probably beat us back.

Hantavirus, an infection transmitted by deer mice, killed several people, including an Indiana man, in the early to mid-1990s. Extreme precautions were recommended when handling their carcasses or cleaning their excrement. Wear rubber gloves and masks and use disinfectant, was the advice. Not certain whether ours were white-footed or deer mice, we could no longer view them as endearing and amusing, though annoying, creatures. We had to eradicate them. That still meant ratcheting up our exclusionary tactics—namely mouse-proofing all the kitchen cabinets and blocking all access. Ha.

Year five. Mouse droppings were under the stove and inside the oven. In our minds we shrank to mouse size and searched for openings top and bottom, back and front, inside and out. Hardware cloth, steel wool, and a wooden bar along the edge of the storage drawer were deterrents. Unfortunately, before that, mice had inhabited the insulated space between the inner and outer oven walls, so that even the full, fruity aroma of cherry cake baking in the oven failed to mask the nauseating stench of mouse. No amount of fresh air carried the rank odor away. We bought a new stove and mouse-proofed it, too. When we trapped mice a day or more before their eventual release to a site several miles away, I fed them rations of raisins, oatmeal, and celery.

Year six. I found mouse droppings under my pillow and dog food in Joe's slipper. A disgusting quantity of mouse droppings had been left under the microwave. Pages of several natural history books were nibbled near a grapefruit-sized nest at the back of a bookshelf. All but one of the several dozen butterfly milkweed seeds, carefully separated from their silks, disappeared. Outwitted still.

Year seven. Another killed in a snap trap. "I'm so sorry," I whispered to no one as I removed it from the wire vise. Cups full of thistle seed were piled and scattered in the utility closet. What had I left unattended? Ah, yes. The seeds in a gallon-sized plastic jug hadn't been transferred to a glass or metal container. Ingenious mice had chewed a small hole near the bottom so that seeds flowed as from an opened spigot like manna from heaven. Guests were coming, and I wanted to clean the cabin, but the vacuum cleaner wouldn't work. I disassembled one part after another until I removed and looked through a flexible tube, or tried to. It was clogged with dog hair and lint from the dust bag. Mice again!

Year eight. Three large holes were chewed in one of Joe's wool sweaters. An inch of fabric around the camera bag zipper was chewed away, and the teeth of the zipper were gone. Mouse droppings and chewed camera instructions littered the bottom of the bag. The cinnamon-scented soap bar was half gone, and what remained was rough from tiny tooth marks. The edge of the braided wool rug, brought from my parents' home, was chewed. I thought all entry points had been plugged, but mouse damage continued.

Year nine. How could mice get into the metal canister filled with sunflower seeds? They did. While I was cleaning the closet, a mouse jumped onto and immediately off my shoulder. Live-trapped three.

Year ten. Birdseed husks and mouse droppings littered the computer printer. Luckily, the mechanics and electronics were undamaged. After ten years of the exclusionary method, mice still lived in my space. With deep reluctance, I put out D-Con. Thus ends this mousy tale—or mouse tail.

# Snakes Alive!

A SNAKE, the diameter of a pencil, slithered from beneath the evergreens toward the deck. It was dark, dull gray with a narrow, bright yellow-orange band across its "neck" and sloughed skin clinging to its tail. Three others followed. One flowed onto the deck where I stood. From a safe distance, I observed these ring-necked snakes through binoculars and admired their good looks.

During most of the World War II years, my parents and I lived in Washington, D.C., where my father was stationed with the Army Air Corps. We often visited the National Zoo, including the Reptile House. Steps made it possible for us little people to view snakes on the other side of glass windows. When the war ended in 1945, we moved to a two-bedroom bungalow, a half-block south of Broad Ripple High School's football field; that was my family's home until 1958. Since 1965, I have lived seven short blocks east of that postwar home. Since 1945, I have seen only one snake in that neighborhood—a garter snake behind the home of a grade-school classmate who lived at the southeast corner of 61st and Rosslyn. Despite my early, benign exposure to snakes, snake phobia plagues me. I cover pictures of them in magazines and books, read the text, and quickly turn to the next page. Even images on the back side of the page make me feel uneasy.

Southern Indiana, including Brown County, has a significant snake population. This region may have as many as ten species, according to Brown County State Park naturalist Jim Eagleman, including copperheads, the state-endangered Kirtland's, and the venomous timber rattlesnake. We are losing some, Jim laments, despite our efforts at protection. He states that some snake species are declining along with frogs, turtles, birds, and other wildlife.

Since 1990, I have seen seven species of snakes in Brown County—milk, rough green, black rat, hognose, ring-necked, midland banded, and garter. Two years passed before I saw the first one. My parents had been with me for a brief visit, during which we talked about snakes, ironically, and the fact that Joe and I had not seen one yet. After they left, I was alone; Joe was in Indianapolis. I went to the utility closet and reached up for a jar of birdseed stored on a shelf above the water heater. At that instant, a large snake dropped to the floor in front of me and escaped to the crawlspace. Dark green with a blue-gray to black pattern, it had been coiled on top of the heater for warmth. I ran shrieking out of the house.

Neighbors comforted me and suggested that, based upon my description, the snake was probably a harmless hognose or puff adder.

Two months later, I was alone again. After a shower, barefooted and wrapped with a towel, I was crossing the darkening bedroom toward the closet for my sweat suit when I noticed something on the floor. Black, slender, and curvy, it was two and a half feet long. For a split second, I thought that a belt had been dropped. SNAKE!!! When you're in trouble in Brown County, you call the sheriff's office, which I did. The dispatcher listened to my story and asked, "Do you have a baseball bat?" "No, why?" "You hit it with a ball bat," she replied. "My god, no!" I countered. In a reassuring tone, she promised that Jeff Atwood, a conservation officer, would call. Thankfully, he did, and he calmed me down. "It's probably a milk snake or blacksnake. They forage for mice, rats, and chipmunks." (Joe's recent comment about how few mice we'd seen in the cabin resonated.) Jeff continued, "If you can get it up on a shelf, you can grab it and toss it out the door." That night, to protect me from snakes, I coaxed Cassie onto the futon in the front room where I slept, far from the odious bedroom. The next day Joe came and built an impenetrable one-inch-thick three-sided case around the water heater. Snakes could still come up from the crawlspace through a small floor opening and coil up on the water heater, if they wished, but at least the case blocked their entry into the cabin.

Three years passed before my next, and last, encounter with a snake inside the cabin. The tail end of a black snake, pressed against the wall above the switch plate by the back door, got my attention. Its languid curves followed the right edge of the doorframe as its head reached toward the screen door. Calmly I moved to the front window and shouted down to Joe in my most emphatic you'd-bet-ter-do-something-about-it voice: "There's a snake in the cabin!" Joe responded immediately and came to my aid. I shouted instructions to him from the front deck. Unfortunately, he looked down instead of up and didn't see the snake. In his gentle, patient voice he said, "It's gone," as he opened the screen door and went out. Buffered by the snake's body, which was then draped over the top of the door, it shut softly behind him. When Joe reopened the door, the snake fell. He studied it and noted its twenty-eight-inch length and its diameter, about as big around as his thumb. Then he released it halfway down to the valley. We surmised that the snake had probably fallen from the attic through a trap door with a defective latch into the guest room closet. We repaired the defective latch on the door soon afterwards.

The black rat snake is the most common snake in our region. Although it will eat the eggs of nesting birds, including those of our cherished bluebirds, it does help control the rodent population and is food for other predators. Perhaps another snake that Joe held up, longer than he was tall, was the same one that had flowed from the meadow like a meandering stream, crossed over the path and a wood beam, and disappeared into the perennial bed, where a five-lined skink turned and fled.

I appreciate Sue Hubbell's message in *A Country Year* about humans' intervention with wildlife:

As a human being I am a great meddler; I fiddle, alter, modify. This is neither good nor bad, merely human, in the same way that the snake who eats mice and phoebes is merely serpentish. But being human I have the

kind of mind which can recognize that when I fiddle and twitch any part
of the circle there are reverberations throughout the whole.

Her words certainly mirrored my feelings after I fenced my perennial garden with a black plastic netting called Deer-X. The purpose
of the fence was to protect flowers, but the unanticipated, unwanted
result was that it caused the deaths of at least two creatures. Two
snakes became fatally ensnared in the fencing. The first was a three-
foot-long midland banded water snake that got caught in a wadded
mass of fine but tough plastic netting that was hidden by a two-
year accumulation of leaves, dirt, and debris. After I spotted it, Joe
extricated it, noted the markings, and buried the remains. "Could
there be more?" we asked as turkey vultures swooped nearby, smell-
ing carrion. We located what they were sensing—a black rat snake,
also entangled in a lethal ball of netting, cooking in the hot sun. I
had tweaked the environment, and reverberations were being felt.
After that bad day, I used a utility knife to cut off the top and
bottom edges of the entire length of fencing. No flying creature,
such as a butterfly, could be trapped in an upper fold, and no ground
creature, such as a snake, could be ensnared again in those pesky
one-inch plastic squares. That, unfortunately, is not the end. We
draped Deer-X over newly planted boxwood shrubs to keep them
from being further deformed by unidentified nibblers. I hadn't envisioned snakes crawling through plants next to the house. Then
Cassie alerted us to a snake caught in the netting, some of it dangling to the ground. After Joe cut the netting from the snake's neck
and carried the limp creature to the edge of the woods, it turned
onto its back, exposed its light underside, and was still. Disconso-

late, we thought it was dead, not knowing that the snake was a hognose feigning death. (I understand that they may even leave their mouths open with their tongues hanging out, making the "death" pose more convincing.) When we next looked, it had slithered away, having successfully fooled us.

A year or more may pass without my seeing a snake. That may be more alarming and ominous, in a sense, than finding one warming itself on the water heater, hunting prey on the bedroom floor, or hanging out on the wall! As I learn more about snakes, I can at least value them for their importance in the greater scheme of life—and even observe their behavior, from a distance, with binoculars.

C Carlson 04

# Teeming with Life

T HE WORD "MEADOW" comes from Middle and Old English for "mow." The first meadows were mowed by the mouths of grazing animals. While a pasture is a grassland or field that is continuously grazed, a meadow may be a grassland that is cut periodically for hay. I have an eighth-of-an-acre meadow that, in today's vernacular, is a naturalized planting of flowers and grasses in a sunny, open area and is mowed annually. This little meadow became the centerpiece of our creative energies, our joy, while Joe was alive, and it continues to fascinate me. It nods a welcome greeting from both sides of the drive as I turn from the ridge road.

Neil Diboll, the founder of Prairie Nursery in Wisconsin, is a vital force in the prairie restoration movement, an effort shared by millions who want to bring back more of the natural grasslands that once stretched between the forests of the eastern United States (a demarcation that meandered through Indiana) to the slopes of the Rocky Mountains. The grassland concept is being duplicated throughout the Midwest on a lesser scale. Neil professes that if you like surprises, you'll like meadows. I would add that if you are comfortable with chaos, you'll like a meadow. If orderliness is at your core, a meadow may not be for you.

Our meadow had been a traditional lawn. The first spring, we admired the bright green lawn dotted with yellow dandelion flowers and the white puffs of seeds—the scourge of well-mannered lawns —that followed. When the lawn grasses grew and set seed, we wondered how to deal with this ragged expanse without a mower.

My lawn-keeping mentor was my father, who was obsessive-compulsive about his lawn, which he insisted be weed-free and un-blemished. His example, plus advertisements for flawless green carpets of specialty grass achieved with generous doses of chemicals, influenced my attitude—before Joe. While I dug violets from my lawn and consulted experts about getting rid of nimbleweed, dandelions, crabgrass, and other undesirables, Joe was scattering clover seeds for an interesting and pollinator-friendly lawn.

In 1991, I purchased Laura Martin's *Wildflower Meadow Book* about meadow gardening, prairies, and a movement in the Midwest to undertake prairie restorations that led to the creation of a popular landscape design adaptable to the home garden. Martin's ideas altered my perception of good gardening.

In the section on flower species, I checked those that might grow in south-central Indiana. I dreamed, as gardeners do, about my future Brown County garden, a naturalized planting. I stirred black-eyed Susan seeds from my Indianapolis garden into the soil, and the next summer they were a golden greeting along the drive. Ox-eye daisy and white yarrow appeared spontaneously amid the dozen or more species of grass. I introduced seeds of blackberry lilies, Queen Anne's lace, and butterfly milkweed and lounged among the blooms of the tall purple-top grasses that swayed in the breeze.

Kay Yatskievych, author of *Field Guide to Indiana Wildflowers*, spoke to the Horticultural Society of the Indianapolis Museum of Art in the winter of 1992 about her book, which was then in process. She lamented to a small group afterwards that Indiana was the only state east of the Mississippi River without a native plant society. At the time I didn't know what a "native plant" was, but obviously Indiana should have such a society, so I announced, "I'll call a meeting." A year passed. On February 26, 1993, eight inches of snow fell, and Bill Brink, with a borrowed four-wheel-drive vehicle, was the only one who could get to the first meeting with Joe and me in our Broad Ripple home. Even intrepid Carolyn Harstad, who would later write *Go Native!*, was snowbound. Nevertheless, the Indiana Native Plant and Wildflower Society (INPAWS) was born.

Through INPAWS I learned that native plants are plants that grew here naturally before European settlement. They are the wild-flowers that sparkle in our forests in the spring before the trees leaf out and block the understory plants from sunlight; goldenrods and asters, known by some as field flowers; the prairie flowers and grasses that grew in the great grasslands that flowed uninterrupted from western Indiana to the Rocky Mountains. They are the flowers, ferns, trees, and shrubs that, along with insects, birds, and other forms of wildlife, evolved together. They adapt to the whims of nature and survive the vagaries of Indiana's weather—March and April cold snaps, drenching rains, and summer droughts. They don't need much help from us, and that appeals to me. I now use native plants, shrubs, and trees extensively in my urban garden and foster a prairie-type meadow here. The *Indianapolis Star* featured both, a tribute to the beauty and virtue of our pre-settlement heritage.

There are several ways to install a meadow, all well described and documented elsewhere. In the beginning our approach was primarily to wait and see. We simply mowed it once a year in early spring. A trip with INPAWS to Shiloh Pioneer Cemetery, where remnant prairie plants grew, yielded seeds that Joe and I plucked and scattered and that germinated and now grow in my meadow. Occasionally I transplanted natives into the meadow with a vision in mind, a vision that some observers might not understand and that I may never fully achieve.

Harnessing solar power is a good way to sterilize the soil before planting seeds or plugs. The *American Gardener* recommends pinning down doubled sheets of clear plastic (clear plastic permits more heat to pass through it and enter the soil, while black plastic tends to absorb heat) at least two and a half feet wide over trimmed grass or weeds for a season, or through the sunniest, warmest part of the year. Solar heat cooks and kills vegetation under it, leaving a bare, sterile space, ready for desirable seeds to germinate and grow undisturbed and uncrowded for a year or so.

We had an area of tough fescue that seemed too large for us to handle, so a landscaping firm prepared the soil and later planted seeds. After seven unusually cold and windy spring weeks with vast sheets of black plastic pinned down, we lifted the plastic. It was too soon; the fescue and weeds had not "cooked." Undeterred, we had the top few inches of soil turned. Then "Claybuster"—a mix of nine forbs, four legumes, and four grasses—was cast, the soil rolled, and straw spread.

We had been too eager. We should have closely followed some procedure described in reputable literature. Unimaginably dense mats of opportunistic weeds and sprouts from chopped bits of fescue roots soon prevailed. The first seedlings were not prairie plants but rather common and English plantain, ragweed, sour clover, and sedge. I yearned to pull them out, but that would have been foolish and impossible. There were hundreds of thousands of tiny plants. Would desirable seedlings have a chance? Other options were to spray with herbicide or, later, cut the flower heads. I sprayed herbicide on dense patches of fescue and on some other weeds. In spite of that dreadful start and an arid summer, masses of newly seeded black-eyed Susans bloomed in September. Then, in October, the most widespread plant of that year appeared, native Indian tobacco, *Lobelia inflata.* I couldn't bear the idea of millions of their seeds scattering on the receptive bare ground where our seedlings were expected. I attacked with my clippers, cutting off thousands of those little devils until my hand ached. But time was running out, so I used a weed whip. The action of the whirling motorized whip on the plants caused them to release an invisible mist, which caused my throat to close and my lungs to tighten. Frightened by visions of my early demise, I gave up my effort and allowed my throat and lungs to return to normal.

Four years later, the results were good to beautiful. In the fifth, big blue stem and Indian grass began to dominate that portion of the meadow, and flowering plants were disappearing. Some revision will be needed.

After you get a meadow started, you have to maintain it. Burning is regarded as the best way to maximize a meadow's appearance and is advocated over mowing. Most experts, though, recommend burning one-third each year on a rotating basis. This leaves two-thirds of the area unscathed for insects and other inhabitants.

To meadow and prairie managers, February means BURN. And that's what Joe and I did in 1995. On the 23rd, conditions were perfect, and I suggested that we try a little experiment. The plant residue was dry; the wind was light. Pyro Joe leapt to the idea. We began very timidly with a six-by-six-by-six-foot triangle, bounded by the drive, a dampened path, and a band of mowed vegetation. The hose was near. We made the mistake of lighting the fire on the windward side, and it took off. My heart raced as I fanned the downwind side with a broom. I wondered if we should have notified the fire department. I pictured our forest in flames. But we contained the small fire, and it burned itself out. Our first burn was successful.

Buoyed, we moved to an adjoining section the next evening. The drive, the path, the burned area, and a three-foot-wide strip of tarred roofing paper defined that space. We lit the grass from the correct downwind corner for a controlled burn. Then we crossed the drive and burned into the night. By the 25th we had two broad, blackened patches of charred ground. Eager to do more and more, we started another fire a week later. We weren't timid enough, and we lost one broom, one Canadian hemlock, and the orange plastic fence that surrounded it. Also, after we first lit the grass, the water faucet handle fell off as I attempted to turn on the water. In the heat of the moment, pliers solved that problem. Then I noticed the hose stretched across a smoldering area; its outer layer was melting. In spite of our mistakes, that burn was also a success. Two weeks later, no char was visible; it was masked by robust green sprouts.

That summer there were flowers in the meadow, in contrast to four years earlier. There were daisies, yarrow, daisy fleabane, Houstonia, and sweet yellow clover (considered a noxious weed by many). Every day we walked around and through it, excited by its fresh new look. Had the burn caused the dramatic difference, or was it due to the passage of time after cessation of regular mowing? On the Fourth of July, great spangled fritillaries sipped nectar from orange butterfly milkweeds and purple coneflowers. Goldfinches bent English plantain while eating its fresh seeds. Grasshoppers and crickets leapt away when we plunged into tall vegetation for a closer look at dragonflies or to check the progress of prairie grasses and flowers.

In April, after mowing or burning, violets bloom along with a few dandelions, most of which have disappeared, shaded out by tall meadow plants. By May it's time to mow paths through and around the edges. Michael Pollan writes in *Second Nature*, "That path, in my eyes anyway, is a thing of incomparable beauty, especially right after it's mowed. I don't know exactly what it is, but that sharp, clean edge changes everything; it makes a place where there wasn't one before. . . . The path beckons, making the whole area suddenly inviting."

And then comes summertime, when the meadow blooms. Black-eyed Susan, butterfly milkweed, ox-eye daisy, sweet yellow clover, whorled, garden, and lance-leafed loosestrife, wild daylily, fleabane, rough-fruited cinquefoil, spiderwort, yarrow, red clover, Deptford pink, early goldenrod, Queen Anne's lace, purple coneflower, tway-blade orchid, penstemon, liatris, white false indigo, bee balm, nar-row-leafed mountain mint, cup plant, prairie coreopsis, phlox, common marsh pink, St. Johnswort, gray-headed coneflower, prairie dock, prairie false indigo, blackberry lily, lance-leafed and rough-leafed goldenrod, false sunflower, ironweed, ladies'-tresses orchid, field thistle, blue lobelia, and a myriad of grasses and sedges. With the blooms come wood nymphs, sulphurs, great spangled fritillar-ies, swallowtails, dragonflies, bees, and grasshoppers. There's tex-ture and variety. Flies, birds, butterflies, beetles, and bees feast on the pollen produced there and ensure seed set. Bumblebees revel in the frothy beds of Queen Anne's lace, running and tumbling in a zigzag course and gathering pollen all over their fuzzy bodies.

In July, the meadow, at its most glorious, becomes a living testa-ment to my mother, who was devoted to flowers and wildlife. Sadly, she lost her sight late in her life, and she could no longer see the natural world that had brought her such pleasure. On the Fourth of July 2000, the fourth anniversary of her death, I wrote: "I wish Mother were by my side so that I could hold her hand and describe to her the beauty of the meadow. It shimmers with yellow prairie coneflowers and purple coneflowers, while indigo buntings and goldfinches relish floral treats and drink the water collected by the cup plant."

In September, grasses and goldenrods create a golden glow. Asters follow. A young helper here told us that his grandmother called asters "frost flowers." The meadow asters, most likely bushy, calico, and small white, are true to the native species that they are and form an exuberant understory cloud of delicate, airy bouquets, flourishing even when the earth is parched from a summer of drought.

During their fall migration one year, a flock of stunning green Tennessee warblers descended to the meadow and joined a song sparrow and a hummingbird that dipped into a goldenrod blossom. Many flower heads were bare, their seeds plucked by indigo buntings, goldfinches, and others. Fall is a good time of year to carry a chair up the path and sit amid the meadow to observe and write. Stems of purple-top grass, some with purple florescence and some a mature brown, lean and wave to the wind's rhythm, and grass shadows dance across the pages of my journal. At eye level are teasel-like, needle-sharp black seedpods of purple coneflowers; their pointed leaves, rough like sandpaper, take on a purple hue. By the end of October, the meadow slumbers.

In winter the meadow provides nutrients for juncos, song sparrows, American tree sparrows, and secretive small mammals. Erect plants offer a protective habitat for rabbits and other wildlife. Heavy snows may flatten the plants as though they've been crushed by a steamroller. Footsteps on a cold morning sound like you're tramping on giant, crisp shredded wheat biscuits. I await another perfect late February day to mow or burn the meadow and begin the cycle anew. I become suffused with a glorified image of what's to come, eagerly anticipate the plant succession, and picture a greater array of flowers in my naturalized garden than in the years before.

In 1999, a two-week odyssey took me to Colorado and back. A cardboard box rode beside me on the passenger seat. The box was filled with maps, guides, and books about prairies: *PrairyErth*, a study of Chase County, a sparsely populated tract of tall-grass prairie in the Flint Hills of central Kansas; *Tall Grass Prairie*; *Prairie: The Land and Its People*; and *Plain Pictures: Images of the American Prairie*. I had a purpose, and that was to experience prairies. When I pulled into a filling station in Pawhuska, Oklahoma, and asked for directions to the Tallgrass Prairie Preserve, a tract encompassing thirty-eight thousand acres where bison roam again, a paunchy local farmer dressed in overalls offered to lead me. "Just follow my pickup; I'm goin' that way," he said. He motioned me in the right direction, and I drove to the prairie, stopping around 4:30 in the afternoon under the shade of a towering cottonwood tree growing along a meandering stream. The air temperature was a wilting 105 degrees. I guzzled water, lathered my exposed skin with sunscreen, plunked my wide-brimmed straw hat onto my head, opened my umbrella embellished with dark green enlarged images of beech tree leaves, and followed the mowed path. I was soon standing in the prairie. Vivid pink prairie roses and prairie rose gentians, as well as yellow partridge peas, painted my way. Alone and shocked by the heat's intensity, I didn't linger long; nevertheless, I breathed in the prairie's spirit.

The next day I rolled across Kansas, once entirely prairie and now mostly cultivated or grazed by cattle. Massive feedlots abound along historic U.S. Highway 50, and the air reeks from the putrid aroma of cattle crowded together in close quarters. In contrast to that part of Kansas, I drove back through Nebraska's Sand Hills, a region of rich virgin grasslands that cover nearly one-fourth of the state. Finally, I made one more prairie visit—Illinois's Goose Lake Prairie State Park. In mid-August, grasses and forbs were tall, thick, lush, and blooming, and drifts of contented orange and black monarch butterflies floated near and sipped nectar.

Prairies are among the most rare of our natural resources. Their plants grow deep roots and withstand natural adversities—drought, fire, fierce cold, searing heat, and grazing bison. However, most of this diverse landscape could not survive the westward pioneer movement. Beginning with the wave of settlers in the nineteenth century, millions of acres, including Indiana's three million, have been plowed under, overgrazed, or developed. Yet today prairie remnants, those fragments that survive and the prairie meadows that we are reestablishing, whisper to us about the vast midsection of our country a little more than a century ago. Prairie plants stand as a symbol of my own tenacity and survivability.

C Carlson 04

# Uninvited Ungulates

I UNASHAMEDLY SUPPORT HUNTING to reduce deer populations and advocate that hungry hordes of deer be reduced in our state parks. However, on the eve of my major revision of this chapter, the *Brown County Democrat* ran a full-page ad for its new *Brown County Outdoors Hunting & Fishing Magazine*. In the ad a man cradles the severed head of an eight-point buck. That image brought conflicts to the fore that the subject of deer arouses in me and in millions of North Americans who grapple with these beautiful and adaptable ungulates, whether white-tailed, mule, or black-tailed.

A review by Robert Finch in the *New York Times Book Review* section led me to find *Heart and Blood: Living with Deer in America* by Richard Nelson. Finch drew my attention when he wrote that many of us have had direct, and not always positive, interchanges with deer in our gardens, in our crop fields, on our highways, and even on our jet runways. He recommended *Heart and Blood* for its balanced look at the complex relationships between people and deer in our shared homeland. This book, written by a man who regards deer with awe and reverence, includes various perspectives—from biologists, Native Americans, animal rights advocates, hunters, wildlife watchers, farmers, ranchers, land managers, social scientists, and suburban dwellers. It amplified in manifold ways my understanding of the endearing, infuriating, and even dangerous deer that share their land with us humans.

Joe and I had no idea of the impact that white-tailed deer would have on our lives when we began coming to our Brown County property in 1990. The previous owners had established flower beds, and we added to them. White pines and mixed conifers were also planted. But in the spring of 1992, when twelve deer left our young meadow and melted into the north woods as we turned into the drive, we knew a challenge awaited, especially when we discovered that they had browsed tulips, white pine needles and branches, and a patch of wild daylilies ten feet in diameter. Later, in our absence, they devoured hostas, tiger lilies, mountain mint, and pansies. Each time we approached our drive after an absence, my stomach churned, and I braced myself for the damage I knew I would find. The golden sweep of black-eyed Susans I had envisioned near the top of the drive was nipped in the dream stage. The following winter, when several inches of snow blanketed the ground for several days, ravenous deer severely pruned the stand of arborvitae and the white and Norway spruces.

We talked with landscape experts and read magazine and newspaper articles about what to plant, what not to plant, and how to deter deer. We combed Cassie and draped her fur on evergreen branches. We sprayed Tree Guard, a solution that left a sticky residue, which then collected an unattractive film of dust; Tree Guard with red pepper, which clogged the first sprayer we used; and a solution with whole eggs. Nothing worked, including the hunters we invited. In 1994 we erected the first deer exclusion fence, parallel rows of orange construction fencing that we laced onto iron rebars pounded into the earth every three feet. It was remarkably ugly but effective, and it protected our perennial beds. Each time we arrived, we lifted the fencing off the rebars and rolled it up, then reversed the process when we left. We graduated to the black plastic netting called Deer-X. Eventually fencing traced a route through part of the meadow and surrounded the cluster of conifers. Joe's system became more elaborate, with Deer-X, rebars, tree trunks, binder's twine, and boundless determination. He devised makeshift gates—awkward but functional—with long, narrow boards, duct tape, and deck screws to attach to the fencing. This required absurd amounts of energy and time, but our relief and joy increased beyond words. Because of Deer-X, the fence was nearly invisible, was relatively easy for us to pass through, and was inexpensive and effective—or so we thought. Euphoria dissolved when we returned and found bee balm, daylilies, sassafras, sumac, thimbleweed, Queen Anne's lace, and twinleaf seedpods nipped. Bill Krieg, my nephew, reminded me that if deer want to eat something inside your fence, they'll find a way. Nevertheless, we reinforced it by running taut strings through the bottom and top edges. We added a thin cotton string a few feet inside the fence, hoping that if a deer jumped over, its trajectory would carry it into the string, which would then snap, revealing the animal's behavior and entry points.

That fencing system, our third home remedy, failed. So in 1997 a Designscape crew attached seven-foot-wide black polypropylene fencing to twelve-foot-tall rebars positioned along the two sides of the meadow and stapled it to trees where it runs through the forest. Deer can jump eight and a half feet vertically, so the full width of the fencing is adequate where the ground slopes upward; additional wires were added above the fencing where the ground is generally level. There are four gates.

This system has essentially excluded deer from two-thirds of an acre, including the meadow, the perennial beds, the conifers, the natural forest understory, and the cabin. There have been a few exceptions. A young sassafras tree branch, nipped cleanly at an angle, alerted me to a breach, which I soon located. Presumably, the force of a charging deer had ripped a four-foot slit in the fence, leaving a gently flapping entry point, a tear that I easily wove shut with strong braided string.

Recently there was a disconcerting incident. I arrived late at the cabin in the afternoon, in time to grab some food, change clothes, and walk next door to meet my neighbor for a ride to Bloomington, where world-renowned violin virtuoso Joshua Bell was to perform in honor of his late father. Before I left, I noticed something bobbing up and down in the flower garden at the far end. At first I wondered whether it was a squirrel leaping around. Then I saw the big ears, and then the entire face. A deer! It had come in behind me through the open gate! I was astonished. I had assumed they were programmed to walk *around* the fenced area, not *through*. Had I left without seeing the creature, I would have had a rude awakening the next morning. When I approached to shoo the deer out, it did not intuitively retrace its steps, as I had hoped. Instead, it went to an upper corner, turned, followed the fence line, and then bounded over the fence and away, jerking staples and fencing from trees as it fled. Fortunately, the tough plastic fencing material did not rip, and Grover soon repaired the damage.

Because of my fence, I can enjoy the deer as they browse nearby, take a cooling dip in the pond, or bound away with a flash of their showy white tails. The hostility that I once felt is gone. Good fences do make good neighbors.

Before European settlers, there may have been between twenty-five and fifty million deer in North America. In 1890 the U.S. Bureau of Biological Survey estimated that three hundred thousand of them remained in this country. Ten years later the federal government enacted the Lacy Act, which prohibited interstate commerce in game taken in violation of state law—and brought an end to commercial hunting. Bounty hunters were offered rewards for tracking down predators such as wolves, in hope of reversing the alarming decline in deer populations. Aldo Leopold wrote in *A Sand County Almanac:*

> I have lived to see state after state extirpate its wolves. I have watched the face of many a newly wolfless mountain, and seen the south-facing slopes wrinkled with a maze of new deer trails. I have seen every edible bush and seedling browsed, first to anemic desuetude and then to death. I have seen every edible tree defoliated to the height of a saddle horn. Such a mountain looks as if someone had given God a new pruning shear, and forbid-

den Him all other exercise. In the end, the starved bones of the hoped-for
deer herd, dead of its own too-much, bleach with the bones of the dead
sage, or molder under the high-lined junipers. I now suspect that just as a
deer herd lives in mortal fear of its wolves, so does a mountain live in
mortal fear of its deer.

Now, a century later, the population of deer in North America is
between fifteen and twenty-five million, possibly greater than in
the sixteenth century. We are paying the price for the 1900 Lacy
Act; we must be predators again.

By the mid-1880s, deer had been completely eliminated in Indiana. Between 1934 and 1942, 256 deer were reintroduced in Indiana's
state forests and 40 in Brown County State Park. By 1947, 4,000
were estimated statewide. In the mid-1950s, 100 additional deer were
purchased and brought into the state.

A wild deer population can double every two to three years,
and, barring disease and predators, a mating pair can produce twenty
to thirty descendants in ten years. As a result of their pyramiding
reproduction, the progeny of those few hundred deer reintroduced
around the middle of the twentieth century have now grown to
exceed five hundred thousand.

White-tailed males weigh between 130 and 250 pounds, females
between 100 and 180 pounds. Needless to say, these big vegetarians
need a lot of plant material to survive. They thrive on twigs, shrubs,
fungi, acorns, grass, and herbs throughout the year and are considered a major threat to eastern woodlands because trees of the future are nipped as young seedlings. They may live sixteen years in
the wild and do considerable damage to young orchards and vegetable crops if their populations are not controlled. Essentially

unchecked today, deer thrive on suburban and even urban landscape plantings, agricultural crops, botanical gardens, and natural
vegetative growth in public parks and forests. The economic and
biological impact is enormous.

Protectors of large public parks and forestlands do not have the
luxury of erecting exclusionary fences. Reducing herds to the carrying capacity of an area, meaning the number of deer that an area
can sustain and still maintain its integrity, is the answer. The ideal
carrying capacity is eight to ten deer per square mile in a park like
Brown County State Park, where people want to see them, and five
to six per square mile outside of parks. I assume that Joe would
have agreed with those figures when he wrote to the editor of the
*Brown County Democrat* that Indiana does not need "deer parks." What
we do need, he urged, is a public forest teeming with natural flora
and fauna.

He and I promoted serious discussion of the problem in Indiana's
state parks when the Indiana Department of Natural Resources
made a case for culling the deer herd in 1993. The Indiana Native
Plant and Wildflower Society sponsored a program called "Deer
and Indiana's State Parks: Where Have All the Wildflowers Gone?"
A panel of experts presented their perspectives and answered questions. As a result, INPAWS supported the recommendations of
the Brown County Deer Study Committee and the Natural Resources Commission that hunts be held. In those Indiana state parks
that have been hunted, both the vegetation and, consequently, the
wildlife interacting with that vegetation have improved unequivo-
cally.

Back here on Lawson Ridge, I've seen a doe affectionately browsing side by side with her fawn in our north woods, outside the fence. Another time, with my hands full of soft, ripe persimmons that I'd gathered along the roadside, I startled a young deer. It bounded a short distance into the forest, then stopped, studying me. Curious, it pivoted its head, like an owl's, more than 180 degrees, never taking its eyes from mine. I moved on, leaving it to wonder if I was friend or foe. That is the question. You, dear reader, may decide.

# Some Arachnids and Other Distractions

I WRITE ON AND ON about this idyllic place. For me it's nearly perfect, but not absolutely. Nuisances range from the microscopic to the thunderously large.

Consider ticks and chiggers. To those who have had Rocky Mountain spotted fever or Lyme disease, ticks, the vectors for these life-threatening diseases, are viewed as more than a nuisance. To me, these bloodsucking, parasitic arachnids are merely disconcerting. When ticks crawl up my leg, torso, arm, or neck at night, they wake me from deep sleep, tickling my nerve endings en route to my scalp. When one makes it all the way up and attaches itself for a blood meal, I pull it off and usually release it outside. How can one live tick make a difference? I ask. Once, feeling less kindly, I dropped a tick onto the woodstove, and to my astonishment, it walked off the sizzling surface. I have also crushed them with rocks, but I seldom follow the advice to "Flush it down the toilet." What a waste of precious water from my point of view!

Anyone who has camped, lived, or hiked in Brown County in the spring or early summer has encountered one or more of Indiana's tick species, such as these commonly known as the deer, lone star, American dog, black-legged, wood, and brown dog tick. Excluding the egg phase, both male and female ticks need a host to provide a blood meal for each of their three developmental stages—larval, nymph, and adult. They cannot run, hop, fly, or move quickly, so to find a host, they first climb up tall grass, weeds, fences, and even the sides of buildings. Mammals emit biochemicals, such as $CO_2$, and heat. These, as well as vibrations, trigger ticks to assume their "questing" stance. Clinging to vegetation with their rear legs, they position themselves with their front legs extended, waiting to attach themselves to the clothing or fur of a potential host as it brushes against their outstretched legs. Ticks in the larval stage may wait months for this moment to happen. While they are feeding, their outer covering, or cuticle, grows accordion-like to accommodate a large volume of blood—from two hundred to six hundred times their unfed body weight. When full, a tick drops to the ground and, with only the tips of its tiny black legs showing from under its chalky brown burden, toddles away. Following a female adult's final meal, she deposits thousands of eggs in cracks, crevices, or the soil and then dies. (Males also die following the reproductive phase.)

Despite my casual approach to ticks, experts advise that we cover ourselves well with light-colored clothing when outdoors during tick season, examine ourselves or have someone else examine us, and remove an attached tick by grasping its head with tweezers and pulling.

Among other memorable arachnids that lurk in grasses and low vegetation are chiggers. I vividly remember fiercely scratching the welts in my navel, and on other places on my body, during the summers when, as a young girl, I attended the Girl Scouts' Camp Dellwood on the west side of Indianapolis. In June 1992, several decades later, at least one hundred chigger "bites" adorned my body a few hours after a stroll through the low growth in our newly developing meadow. In August of the following summer, after three hours crouched in the young meadow photographing flowers and insects, I was dotted again, head to toe, with masses of red bumps. Now, after thirteen summers, I'm still affected by chiggers, but I seem to have fewer welts that seem less irritating and less prolonged. In contrast, my neighbor's Minnesota grandchildren, Ryan and Amy, required antihistamines for relief from a severe reaction to chiggers. Some friends and relatives, when they share their vivid memories of summertime visits with us, do not immediately recall the cabin, food, conversation, terrain, and birds. Even years later, those pleasantries are obliterated by recollections, indelibly etched into their psyches, of the itching that followed even brief walks on the mowed path through the meadow.

I've not yet seen a chigger, the cause of my itching. Initially, what I learned about chiggers came from Sue Hubbell's *A Country Year*. Unlike chigoe fleas, which inhabit the Deep South and burrow under the skin, chiggers (also called harvest bugs, harvest mites, jiggers, and redbugs) are mites. Only the larval stage needs an animal host. They hatch from minute eggs laid in the soil, crawl up vegetation, and wait for a suitable vertebrate host, including humans, domestic and wild animals (including reptiles), poultry, and wild birds. Since it would take 125 of them lined up snout to rear to make an inch, we cannot see them, and we seldom realize they have been feeding on us until we begin to itch. (According to Hubbell, some folks who live in the Ozarks, where she lived and wrote, swear that the best way to avoid getting "chigger bit" is to conduct one's outdoor activities stark naked. Presumably the chiggers will then wander up one side of the body and down the other, discouraged by finding no suitable spot on which to feed.) Itching occurs after chigger larvae have scurried for a skin pore or hair follicle in a protected spot, pierced the skin, injected a salivary secretion containing powerful digestive enzymes to break down skin cells, and ingested their high-protein meal of liquefied skin and lymph. Approximately four days later, they drop off their host to metamorphose into the nymphal stage.

An effective deterrent, I've heard recently, is a yellow powder called "flowers of sulfur," which is available at pharmacies. Try dusting it on your shoes, socks, and lower pant legs to fend off these creatures (and possibly people, too). Absent this repugnant powder and following possible exposure to chiggers, it is suggested that you take a hot shower or bath, soaping yourself repeatedly, and that you launder your field clothes in hot, soapy water for thirty minutes or expose them to hot sun. Clothing not treated in either of those two ways will still contain chigger larvae to infest your skin. For temporary relief from itching, there are many commercial products that contain a mild anesthetic. The sooner applied, the better, I'm told.

If you've never seen a chigger or you want to test an area for their presence, here's something to try. Place a six-inch square of black cardboard on edge near a likely habitat for chiggers. It's said that the small yellowish or pinkish chiggers, if present, will climb rapidly to the top of the square and congregate there.

Now to larger pests. Over the years, there have been several free-roaming dogs around us. Traditionally, we allow dogs to run free in the country, despite the serious risks connected with this practice. Loose dogs are sometimes stolen, injured, or killed by cars or hunters; others threaten and even attack passersby, people they perceive as intruders. Those around us, however, have sometimes been too friendly. One or two would tag along with us on hikes, come back with us, and then not want to leave. They whined at the doors, scratched at the windows, and tromped through the garden. Joe would tie them to a sassafras tree with a pan of water nearby and leave a phone message for the owners: "This is Joe Ingraham. Your beautiful, friendly dog is tied up in our yard. Please come for it as soon as possible."

We called one sweet, tenacious, exuberant Jack Russell terrier simply Jack. Our jealous dog Cassie barked, snarled, and bared her teeth at him, and once she shot out the door to vent her hostility, only to fall and injure her leg—a humiliating experience. One May night, a violent electrical storm burst upon us with thunder and lightning. Two and a half inches of rain fell in four hours. Cassie, a wimp during storms, curled up on the closet floor in the back study, where she felt warm, dry, and protected. Jack arrived at our cabin that night. Soaked, he begged to come in. Reluctantly I opened the door: "Okay, Jack. In you go." In seconds he found Cassie, who stood up, snarled, and barked. Rebuffed, Jack trotted away and disappeared. Later I found him sleeping on my bed. Cute, I thought. When Cassie ventured into the front room where I was reading, ever-alert Jack bounded from the bedroom to join us. Then the little devil lifted his little leg and peed on the birch bark wastebasket! I grabbed him, shrieked "Out, Jack! Out!" and ejected him back into the wild night, where he whined and ran from window to window, peering in, wet and frightened. Unable to ignore him, I put on my rain cape and boots and, in the torrential rain, went down and opened the basement. "Here's a dry place for you, Jack." Protection from the storm was not what he wanted. What he wanted was companionship, and he trotted back up at my heels. When I went to bed around 10 PM, Jack had his front paws on the sill of the east window, looking in at me. I closed both windows and the sliding glass door so that he wouldn't destroy the screens with his claws. As I fell asleep, he continued to whine and scratch at the bedroom window. In the morning I found him sleeping, curled next to the cabin in the boxwood bed—temporarily a mute nuisance.

Tranquility is relatively elusive in the city. Conversely, my time in Brown County is usually peaceful and treasured. So on those rare occasions when noise rends the air, I feel shaken. When I hear the chainsaw, the fatal crack and muted sound of snapping branches, and the final thud, I wish that trees, like the one across the road that began its life at the time of the Civil War, could be left standing. When drag racers near Bean Blossom rev their engines from sunup to sundown every Sunday from April through October, I wish they would choose a racetrack farther away. When National Guard pilots from Camp Atterbury skim the treetops above me in their mighty jets, I wish they would select someone else's sky to pierce.

That said, and considering the whole, annoyances are few at this, my idyll.

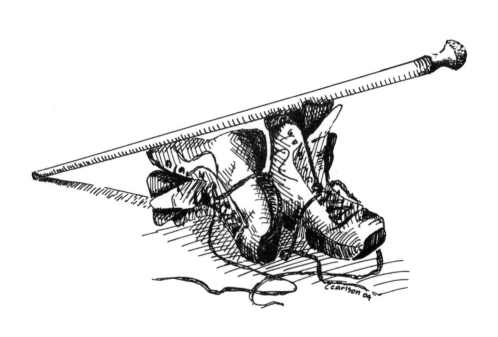

# That's Entertainment

TIME TO SPEND as one chooses is a luxury—even pre-dawn time. Up at 6:00, I started a fire in the stove to ward off the windy, frigid outside air. I made my usual eighteen ounces of French roast coffee, then sat down facing the nearly full moon beaming brightly through the westerly window. Occasionally I had to lift the orange plaid wool blanket from my lap and legs and go the short distance to the stove, where I gave the fire, slow to catch that morning, a shot of oxygen by holding open the ash tray beneath. Back in my viewing chair, my body and mind tensed as the white disc approached the left side of a black walnut trunk, became totally eclipsed, then cast a tiny glimmer on the right side of the trunk until, within a few minutes, the moon fully revealed its mottled self again. On the carpet beside me, moonlight intersected and blended with the faint orange glow cast by the flames that flickered behind me. Though I had drained my cup of coffee, I chose to wait while the moon sank behind the fringe of trees along Annie's Ridge, turned into a coarse lace doily, and vanished.

Entertainment with all its facets spans the breadth of human imagination. Some of us delight in computer games, cruise ships, spectator sports, videos, drag races, fishing, mountain biking, TV game shows, and shopping at the malls. I like to hike, play Scrabble, make maple syrup, listen (and occasionally dance) to WFYI, read books, have dinner in nearby Nashville, cook for friends and family, swim in the pond, cross-country ski, hunt for mushrooms, experience a computer task breakthrough, attend musical performances in Bloomington, photograph flowers and insects, document frogs, drive back roads, watch birds, and, of course, write for entertainment. And now, with structural improvements to the cabin and access to the Internet, I can sit at my computer and, while glancing up to see birds in perpetual motion outside my window, read Sunday's *New York Times* online and, concurrently, receive live transmission of classical music from WQXR in New York City— virtually being in two places at once. My pleasures, diversions, and amusements are endless, the simplest—sipping from a cup of hot coffee as the day dawns or from a glass of wine when the golden light streams through the forest as another day closes.

If I want to immediately connect with the outside world, I turn on WFIU, which informs, elevates, and stirs my senses. I "meet" the famous, the not so famous, and others new to me, including

Arvo Part, contemporary composer of *Kanon pokajanen* and other works. In one day, thanks to radio waves, I listened to Mozart arias and *Sibelius* performed by the Chicago Symphony Orchestra, an interview with opera singer Sylvia McNair, and a discussion of educator Aldous Huxley. Another morning, I heard about federal land swaps, a nineteen-thousand-ton heavy oil spill off Japan, the slaughter of bison in Yellowstone, abnormalities in Florida alligators, and the fact that DDT is still manufactured and used. That afternoon I listened to a reading of Hans Christian Andersen's *Thumbelina* and songs by Indiana's Cole Porter.

During the first six years, Joe's old black and white TV was rolled out of the closet an average of once every other year—one of those times to watch Christy's high school alma mater, tiny Jesuit Brebeuf Preparatory School, attempt to defeat powerhouse Gary Roosevelt in Indiana's basketball finals, and another to witness a Clinton/ Dole presidential debate.

We liked to read aloud the "Sheriff's Log" printed weekly in the *Brown County Democrat* (and occasionally read by David Letterman on his late-night show). We laughed until we cried. These from 1995:

> January 11, 9:22 A.M. "Officer wants the dispatcher to call a woman because her cow is out on Salt Creek Road."

> January 16, 1:03 P.M. "South Shore Drive woman says she knows who has been sitting in her driveway. It is her cousin, but she doesn't know his name."

> January 24, 3:31 P.M. "Woman complaining that a sheriff's deputy drove past a motorist who needed help then did not use turn signals."

January 28, 2:48 P.M. "Sweetwater caller reports a boat is in the lake and can not tell if anyone is in the boat." 3:07 P.M. "Officer says the boat is frozen in the lake. Nothing can be done until the big thaw."

February 9, 1:06 P.M. "Gatesville Road woman says someone is in the woods yelling for help." 1:09 P.M. "Woman says it is a goat in heat."

5:24 P.M. "Harsh Road man wants help because several horses are submerged in a lake. People are holding its head above the water." 5:35 P.M. "Man says they have gotten horses out of the lake."

As the years elapsed, Joe and I devoted ever-increasing time and attention to our immediate environs, but in our early years we often explored the county on foot and by car. We hiked the Trail of the Americas, maintained for use by the Boy Scouts but pleasant for others of us, too. Turn left at the top of our drive and you're on this trail that winds through Youngman Woods Nature Preserve and "T's" at a crossroad where a general store once existed in what is now deep, sparsely populated woods. Go right to Clay Lick Road or left past Wallow Hollow to Bear Wallow Hill, where bears once made depressions in the clay which, when combined with their shed fur, formed a sort of cement and held water to cool them during hot summer months. It is said that in earlier times, Bear Wallow Hill was known as Tepee Mountain, where the legendary Indian Old Kind-Eye spent his final years. Curving on toward the west is Freeman Ridge Road, which meanders through the Nature Conservancy's Hitz-Rhodehamel Preserve, known for its chestnut oak woods and diverse understory plants, and leads eventually to picturesque State Road 135.

On a nippy first day of January, Joe, Cassie, and I hiked the Trail of the Americas. Cassie covered three or four times the distance that we did. Lured by enticing scents, she disappeared from view, tracing giant circles in the woods. Fearing that she might become lost, we called, shouted, clapped, and whistled until we heard snapping twigs, rustling leaves, and the jangle of her dog tags as she raced back, tongue lopping, to join our human gait. The fallen trees that blocked our path forced us to clamber over some, to skirt around others, and to duck-walk under those that had fallen but were still held up partially by erect live trees, spanning the path at odd angles. Clear to pale pink and pale yellow icicles hung from some of the old and porous toppled trees and provided us with arboreal wintertime treats in a range of flavors—hickory, maple, cherry, and oak.

With relatively accurate maps in hand, we drove Brown County's back roads. We headed left on then-graveled Clay Lick to a "T," and from there chose to continue on either Upper Salt Creek or Old Georgetown Pike. If we wanted fresh produce from the now-shuttered, oft-painted and photographed corner store in Bean Blossom, we headed left on the latter. From Bean Blossom, the artistic home of bluegrass music's Bill Monroe, we continued westward to explore the northwestern region of the county—Helmsburg, where a century ago the Illinois Central Railroad delivered artists, salesmen, and others, who then hired a buckboard from the livery stable to take them the rest of the way to Nashville. The railroad was built by a Mr. Calvert, who was memorialized by the next stop on the rail line, the tiny town of Trevlac ("Calvert" spelled backwards). Other times we headed southward on SR 135, gazing from Brown County's ridges at some of the county's expansive, tree-covered vis-

tas before angling onto either Greasy Creek Road or Grandma
Barnes Road, both of which circuitously led us into Nashville.

Sometimes we turned right onto Clay Lick and then east toward
Gnaw Bone, where you can feast on the pork tenderloin sandwiches
recently made famous by being featured on the *Today Show*. Still
following SR 135, we drove down to one-hundred-fifty-year-old
Stone Head, a carved, painted man's head atop a cement mileage
post. Stolen in 1974, it was found in Indianapolis, serving as a hat
rack, and returned. It is the only one of three Stone Heads remaining. The road makes a right angle there and skirts the fertile agrar-
ian valley to Story. Re-energized by a stop for a late breakfast of
banana walnut pancakes at the Story Inn, we proceeded along more
twisting, less-traveled back roads to once-thriving Elkinsville, now
at a dead end and isolated by the nearby lapping waters of Monroe
Reservoir, a haven for boaters, swimmers, and fishers.

Back at the cabin, the idea of making maple syrup began with
Roger Phillips's suggestion in *Wild Food* to tap black walnut trees for
syrup. At the Maple Syrup Festival in Parke County, Indiana, one
February 23, we had mentioned our interest in tapping our walnut
tree to Archy Foxworthy, an old-timer poet and maple syrup maker.
Archy gave us an aluminum spile with instructions to drill a three-
inch hole with a three-eighths-inch bit at an upward angle above a
major root. "No water otherwise. Have a freeze at night, a warm
sunny day, and it'll run. Thirty to forty gallons of sugar water'll
give ya a gallon of syrup," he said. Five days later, on February 28, it
was warm and sunny following a cold night. The experiment began. We decided to start more traditionally, with a maple rather
than a black walnut. As soon as the hole was drilled, sugar water

began to drip. We boiled the water down to syrup on the woodstove. Since we didn't use electricity, the heat was free. The next morning, we poured a little of our first cup of sweet, honey-colored syrup over buckwheat pancakes hot off the woodstove griddle. Delicious!

Local stores didn't sell spiles, the small tubes or spouts inserted into trees to conduct sap, so Joe laboriously carved one from wood to tap our black walnut. Once the spile was in place, the sap ran at a slow trickle, compared to the flow from the maple, and the end product was different. Gelatinous, translucent lumps formed and wouldn't dissolve into the pool of thin syrup. In spite of that, I preferred the flavor of black walnut syrup to maple.

Black walnuts and hickory nuts were abundant in 1995. One Sunday afternoon, while feathery snowflakes whirled around our cabin, I husked them at the kitchen counter. Only three hickories were edible. The unhusked walnuts filled half a grocery bag and weighed eight pounds. With a concrete slab for a solid base, I held the walnuts with a gripping wrench and pounded and pounded and pounded. Some flew up whole and bounced off the upper cabinets; others shattered and flew—just flew. Around 2:00 in the afternoon, Joe, my personal wine steward, presented me with a glass of Beaujolais Nouveau, an ideal accompaniment for the task. At 6:00, with the counter and floor cleaned of the enormous mess, the job was finished. Eight pounds (eighteen nuts per pound) yielded four cups of high-quality nutmeats. What should we do with a quart of black walnuts? Candy was Joe's choice. *Joy of Cooking*'s only listing was chocolate black walnut cake. My other cookbooks didn't list black walnut anything. But Roger Phillips did, suggesting black walnut fudge and ice cream. We chose fudge. It was delicious.

If persimmons aren't ripe when you eat them, your mouth feels dry and puckery. When ripe, these orange fruits, the size of a ping-pong ball, hit the ground with a plop—soft, gooey, and sweet. It's time to make persimmon pudding. My best friend in grade school was Ann Bradford. Back in the 1940s and 1950s, she had relatives with a cabin above Clay Lick. Sometimes I came down with the Bradfords to visit their relatives, and we gathered persimmons, which Ann's mom, Betty, made into pudding back in Indianapolis. (Her recipe has been in my file box ever since.) Persimmon trees grow a few feet from the back corner of the cabin, and five or six grow along the road, but the crop is unpredictable. Some years I have gathered enough for pudding from my tiny grove; other years there are few fruits to none. After watching a raccoon amble up from the woods one afternoon and forage for persimmons, I better understood why I may find few. Others get them first.

Scrabble is my favorite game. Saved tallies, dated and with players identified, go back to February 17, 1993. Joe holds the single game record of 354 points. Christy found an old Scribbage set in our collection; that game ranks second among our favorites. Third is Farkle, an often raucous multigenerational game that Lisa, Christy, and I learned on a windjammer cruise, abbreviated due to fog, out of Mystic, Connecticut. Even my mother, who suffered from Alzheimer's, played. With considerable coaching, she won often, cheered by her "opponents."

In the heart of Peaceful Valley is the small town of Nashville, three miles southwest of my cabin as the crow flies. On the southwest corner of Nashville's main intersection, with the town's only stop-and-go light, is the Hob Nob Corner Restaurant, a former

## BETTY BRADFORD'S PERSIMMON PUDDING

Press persimmons through a colander or Foley food mill.

Dissolve 1 tablespoon of soda in 1 quart of persimmon pulp. Blend in 2 eggs, 2 cups of flour, 1 teaspoon of salt, and 1 cup of sugar creamed with 1 tablespoon of butter. Gradually add 6 cups of milk.

Pour into a large container (I use a large ovenproof bowl) and bake for 3 hours in a 250 degree oven, stirring the mixture occasionally during the first hour.

*Serves 24.*

In my family, persimmon pudding is traditionally served with a dollop of this hard sauce: 1 cup of powdered sugar gradually added to and blended with 5 tablespoons of butter (beaten until soft) and 2 teaspoons vanilla.

drugstore where locals and tourists mingle. The menu seldom changes, and the food preparation is consistently good. It offers something for everyone, whether vegetarians or meat eaters like my father, who loved the liver and onions topped off with a chocolate soda that spilled over the top and ran in sticky streams down the outside of the glass. The Artist's Colony Restaurant is another favorite, with its Shaker-style furnishings, original art festooning the walls, and wood burning in the capacious fireplace on cold days and nights. Their home-style comfort-food cooking, especially their chicken pot pie and baked sweet potatoes with brown sugar sauce, always makes me a happy diner. Tucked here and there in this quaint and historic town are other little restaurants with made-from-scratch food and small shops that feature locally produced arts and crafts in the long-standing artisan tradition of Brown County. There are two art galleries, a bookstore, and the Brown County Playhouse with its well-reviewed theatre productions. Nashville is a nice place to amble, browse, dine, buy, and be entertained.

After Joe died, I pulled myself together on a cold November evening and made my tenuous entry into Brown County's local culture. I had read the *Brown County Democrat*'s headline, "Stringbean Stringband to Reunite," with an accompanying photo of Dave Gore and seven others. "The Stringbean Stringband, 25-year Reunion Concert, 8 PM, November 15, Brown County Inn." Expecting concert seating, I left early to get a place near the front. Outside the door to the "performance hall" was a table, where I paid a ten-dollar cover charge. The back of my hand was stamped, and I walked in—to a dark, shadowy, smoke-filled, low-ceilinged room set up with tables and chairs and packed with boisterous Brown Countians. The stage was at the far end, and the bar was set up in an adjoining room to my left. Had I made a mistake? A lanky couple occupied the table in front of me, and I asked if the other chairs were reserved. "No," they said, so I removed my down jacket and sat down. People continued to crowd through the door immediately behind me. I wondered whether there was an occupation limit, and, if so, whether anyone enforced it. I concluded maybe and no.

The crowd was young, much younger than I. Had I misread the article? Had I bumbled into a twenty-fifth class reunion? My eyes burned from the cigarette smoke. Two attractive barmaids with tiny trays somehow squeezed their way between the tables and people and took drink orders. How they made it back with the correct match was a mystery.

Local singer Frank Jones opened the show at 8:00 PM, but the noise level of the audience didn't abate. I had never attended a performance where the audience drowned out the amplified sound of the entertainer. I tried but could not hear his words. Then I saw Dave half a room away. Okay, I'll stay the course, I concluded. Finally, the Stringbean Stringband mounted the stage. They were introduced and began to play. I was enchanted by their music—the beat, their skill, and their spirit. And I knew one of the stars! In the narrow floor space between the stage and the first tables, people, mostly women, danced. They knew the rhythm and responded. (When Dave called to thank me for my congratulatory note, he said, "If Joe had been there, he would have been out there dancing too." Dave was correct.) The crowd never stopped their conversations; nevertheless, they applauded and cheered at the end of each number.

Over the years, friends and family members have come to the cabin to share in my kind of Brown County–style entertainment. Visitors to this precious hideaway have come from Japan, Kyrgyzstan, and fifteen U.S. states, coast to coast. Some, first-generation U.S. residents, left China, Algeria, and Bosnia, their places of birth, to create a life here in Indiana—as immunologist, computer scientist, hydro-engineer, and researcher in genomics. They represent Joe's family and mine, Joe's university colleagues, my friends and their spouses from grade school, high school, college, and even a Montana dude ranch, Broad Ripple neighbors, members of INPAWS,

staff of OAR-Marion County, members of my Trailing Arbutus
Garden Club, colleagues from long-ago days with the Indiana State
Chamber of Commerce, past associates of First Congregational
Church, and even one Elderhostel study group. They have been
minister, World War I pilot, World War II WAC and WASP, psy-
chiatrist, psychologist, microbiologist, author, poet, artist, graphic
designer, physician, community volunteer, nurse, ceramist, geologist, salesman, teacher, mortician, computer engineer, electrician,
feline veterinarian, waitress, quarryman, university administrator,
social worker, non-profit executive, postal worker, herpetologist,
and botanist.

Lisa, who had been living in Taiwan for several years, returned
to Indianapolis in December 1990 by way of Hawaii, Hong Kong,
China, Russia (via the Trans-Siberian Railway), and Eastern Europe. Two years later she decided to move to Pennsylvania, to join
her future husband. Shortly before departing, she visited Joe and
me here for what I knew would be the last time for many, many
months. The three of us played Scrabble, hearts, and euchre. We
baked and ate copious amounts of onion/cottage cheese bread—
most of two large loaves in twenty-four hours! She explored the
environs and found a delicately constructed vireo nest. Later we
examined mushroom spores through Joe's microscope. It was a bittersweet visit.

I believe that my mother's passion for beauty and nature passed
through me to my own daughters. Lisa and Christy were both with
me in 1998 to help prepare the plaster-dust-coated rooms and furnishings in the cabin for a gathering of the Native Plant Society's
board members and their families. Surely my mother walked with
Lisa when she went into the meadow with clippers, snipped flowers

and grasses, rounded up vases, and created appealing arrangements to delight the eyes of our guests. Mother was also with Christy, a former camp counselor, who took one of the children that day on a walk to see what they could find. They discovered a small box turtle, which they brought up to show us before returning it to the dam.

Typically, guests and I watch the birds feeding, walk to the pond and valley, relish gourmet meals, and hold lingering conversations about the environment, religion, politics, books, families, jobs, marital relations, life, death, and international cultures. As I learn more about Japan's congestion and tendency to overbuild, leaving little that's natural, I appreciate the awed reaction of my friend Toshi Takeuchi from Kyoto as he, Lorraine Gray, and I drank coffee one morning, listening to classical music and gazing into the snow-dusted forest. In a subdued voice he said, "It's a little bit of heaven." That was *before* a line of stately wild turkeys marched up the nearby slope, the only activity at that moment in a landscape lightly touched by man.

That was not Toshi's first trip to Brown County. He was sponsored by the same program that had sent Liao to us—the Council of International Participants, which facilitated exchanges of professionals in human services—and he was our houseguest during part of his stay in Indianapolis. On a sunny September day, Toshi rode down to the cabin in a bulbous beige Cadillac, the car beloved and pampered by my 94-year-old father, a retired Air Force colonel. My father was like many Americans who had lived through World War II and instinctively demonized the enemy—all Japanese people, past and present. But when these two men met at our home in Indianapolis, they quickly buried past history. They clicked.

Together in Brown County, we shared a meal, swapped stories, laughed, and played spirited games of Farkle before my father returned to his home, leaving Toshi with Joe and me. Before the three of us left the next day, the two men paddled like gleeful kids around our tiny pond in a cramped two-person inflatable boat. I have the pictures to prove it.

It was important for my parents to come here. It was their getaway, if only for part of a day. I believe that no one has enjoyed visits to our Brown County cabin more than they. My mother was a lady, and even though her emotions were stunted by Alzheimer's disease, she always thanked us and told us what a lovely time they had had. Despite her blinded eyes, she would turn toward Joe and me and smile slightly; then, as their Cadillac turned up the drive, with her right arm turned sideways and fingers pointed upward, she would wave regally, with her hand swinging slightly from her wrist. Her farewells seemed tinged with melancholy and finality.

Elnura Usupora is my friend from Kyrgyzstan. An inquisitive, articulate young woman who speaks four languages, Elnura grew up in a tiny village in that little-known country that shares borders with Afghanistan and China. She was a student at Indiana University–Purdue University Indianapolis when we met. Disembarking from the same airplane at the Baltimore-Washington Airport, we discovered that we both lived in Indianapolis, and we hastily exchanged phone numbers and e-mail addresses before heading our separate ways. Before she departed five months later, we got together a few times, including Easter Sunday, when Christy picked her up at her multi-story dorm and drove her down to see Brown County. Ahead of us technologically, Elnura captured the cabin and the landscape with her digital camera and sent us photos later via e-mail.

It was easy to pepper her with questions about her culture and beliefs. But when she turned the tables on us? Not so easy. She stumped us when she asked in all seriousness, "Why does a bunny deliver eggs on Easter?" Now that she is back in her homeland working as a translator, Yahoo keeps us connected, though we're half a world apart.

When I have guests, I usually bring with me some clipped and photocopied recipes from my files, as well as cookbooks—*Tassajara*, *Moosewood*, and *New Basics* among many favorites. Tapioca pudding was the dessert requested time after time by my father, who said that it was called "bullet pudding" during his military career in World War I. I have prepared numerous gourmet meals in this isolated bit of rusticity. High on the list of soups are cream of artichoke, tomato-lime-tortilla, lentils monastica, blueberry, and chick pea with spinach. Tantalizing entrees include green peppers stuffed with pork and fruit, penne pasta with shiitake mushrooms and sage pesto, cold pasta with curry and shrimp, salmon with lemon-lime-cilantro sauce, rigatoni with Swiss chard and black bean sauce topped with chopped fresh tomatoes, and lamb moussaka. Desserts? I've served Texas sheet cake, fresh ginger pound cake, orange à l'Arabe, chocolate-amaretti torte, raisin rum bread pudding, and cold lemon soufflé. I do share recipes.

Tuning in to music, hiking through the woods, cruising back roads, harvesting, preparing, and eating wild foods, sampling local cuisine, listening to local entertainers, delving into books, welcoming friends. That's entertainment—Brown County style.

ccarlson 04

# . . . Forest for the Trees

For most of us, Brown County equates to tree-covered hills. Trees in delicate shades of chartreuse, cream, magenta rose, and salmon hail spring's arrival. Six months later they trumpet winter's approach in vibrant and gutsy gold, orange, and red. Every year, hundreds of thousands of tourists stream into the county to view its scenery and enjoy its forested tranquility.

Brown County is in the Highland Rim Natural Region, Brown County Hills Section. Mike Homoya writes in *Orchids of Indiana* that the Brown County Hills Section is characterized by deeply dissected uplands underlain by siltstone, shale, and sandstone. Ravines and lower slopes are dominated by species such as American

beech, red oak, and white ash, while the upper slopes have an almost pure stand of oak, particularly chestnut oak. The understory,
carpeted with grass-like sedges, is typically thick, with tangled,
thorny green brier (a favored food of deer) and low-growing shrubs
such as spicebush.

The Wisconsin glacial maximum occurred between twenty thousand and fourteen thousand years ago, when the glaciers were at
their maximum extent. The southward movement stopped just a
few miles north of my property near the northern boundary of
what, since 1836, is known legally and politically as Brown County.
The glacier scoured the land flat to the north of that edge and left
rich till soils. Not so the land to the south in Brown County. Glacial waters carved streams and riverbeds into the stone deposits in
this south-central Indiana area, forming hilly terrain with narrow
ridges, steep slopes, and narrow, V-shaped valleys—our characteristic dissected uplands. About these "everlasting hills," Henry H.
Gray reminds us in *The Natural Heritage of Indiana* that this landscape
is just the latest page in a book not yet complete, and that some
future geologic event will destroy or bury it and begin a new chapter in Indiana's geology.

These hills, as well as the flatlands of the area now known as
Indiana, were densely forested between 1400 and the 1700s, when
Native Americans lived here. They used fire to manage the forests
and grew corn in the openings. Beginning in the early 1800s, when
it is estimated that there were twenty million acres of forest in
Indiana, individual European settlers, in order to survive, began
clearing the land at the rate of nine acres per year, using some of
the logs for cabins, farm buildings, and split rail fences. There was

more timber than the settlers could use, so a common practice in this hilly area was to cut the trees, shove them into the valleys with workhorses, and set them on fire. Woodpiles and massive tree trunks burned year round, earning Brown County the name "Little Smokies." Early settlers grew corn, raised hogs, and hunted their newly acquired land. While crops grew on cleared ground, hogs, their ears notched and clipped for identification, roamed freely, feeding on fallen acorns and hickory nuts. The practice of allowing livestock to graze in woodlands continued into the 1940s, resulting in a significant loss of understory plants.

By 1900, only three million acres remained of the original twenty million acres of forest that had thrived a century earlier in Indiana. In Brown County, shallow soils were damaged, and devastating erosion followed. Families survived on subsistence farming; many destitute farmers relied on hunting and trapping to make a living. Otto Ping and Frank Hohenberger took compelling photographs of the landscape and folk culture of those sparse times. Pictures taken by these two men are displayed in various buildings in Nashville and have been featured in many books. They help me visualize what life here was like back then.

T. C. (Theodore Clement) Steele was a renowned Hoosier painter who died in 1926. Like photographers Hohenberger and Ping, he recorded images of the Brown County of seventy-five to one hundred years ago, but oil paint was his medium and bucolic landscapes his theme. Selma Steele, his second wife, wrote about life here, theirs and their neighbors', beginning in 1907, when they purchased land near Belmont, a small post office hamlet between Nashville and Bloomington, and built a studio-home (now an Indiana

State Memorial). Her words are published in *The House of the Singing Winds.*

For their first view of the tract of land that was to become theirs, the Steeles took an Illinois Central train from Indianapolis to Helmsburg, and then a hack over a road of deeply rutted mud, stopping for the night in Nashville, a "quaint and charming" town of 350 people. After a similarly difficult eight-mile ride the next day, they walked the final uphill portion in ankle-deep mud.

Selma was impressed by the fact that Brown County was so near a university center (Indiana University in Bloomington), yet the countryside, where travel was slow and very difficult, was untouched by the progress of the world outside the hills. There was no compulsory school attendance. Intermarriage and child marriages were common. Women churned their own butter, wove rag rugs on looms, and cooked meals that consisted primarily of fried foods, hot soda biscuits, and pies. Everybody liked "fat meat"—the fat side of pork pickled in a barrel of brine and prepared thus: "soak it in cold water, drain, roll in flour, and fry in a hot skillet." Families had apple orchards and grew a limited array of vegetables, but no more than they needed for themselves. Clearly, life then was limited and difficult. Tired of passing over roads of gullies and shelves of rocks, Selma advocated road improvements, as well as better schools, but the "natives" countered that such betterments would result in increased taxation, thus making living conditions harder than ever for them.

By 1920, ninety percent of Indiana's forests had been converted to farms, cities, towns, and roads. Highway improvements came to Brown County in the early 1920s, and by 1922 it was possible to haul logs, railroad ties, and sawn lumber out of the county by truck. Commercial sawmills were established in several valleys, and to help pay taxes and support their families, many farmers began to harvest their remaining timber, to the dismay of Brown County's recently arrived artists, such as Steele and Adolph Shulz.

Various upland ridges in southern Indiana earned the special designation of "ten-year" land. During ten years of tillage by the customary methods, so much of the soil washed away that further tillage was unprofitable. Beginning in the 1920s and continuing through the 1930s, the state acquired land for state forests and state parks. This region was in dire economic straits by the 1930s. In 1931, a survey of game animals and environmental conditions by Aldo Leopold highlighted the significant problems of land abandonment and soil depletion. In 1935, Indiana and the federal government agreed to establish the Hoosier National Forest in the southern uplands, and southern Indiana land was purchased from owners anxious to divest themselves of acreage that was no longer productive for agriculture. Today there are few pockets of uncut original forest. The two best-known tracts of old-growth timber are the Pioneer Mothers Memorial Forest in the Hoosier National Forest near Paoli and Donaldson's Woods in Spring Mill State Park near Mitchell. (Other significant stands remain in McCormick's Creek and Turkey Run State Parks.)

President Franklin D. Roosevelt established the Civilian Conservation Corps to put men back to work following the Great Depression. They planted pines and spruce on the new national and state lands to help hold the soil, and they introduced black locust and walnuts on the barren acreage. Other hardwoods sprouted from the existing seed bank. Most private areas returned to woodlands through natural succession. Brown County's public and private lands are once again abundantly forested.

Across the road from my cabin is a camp owned by the Catholic Youth Organization of the Indianapolis Archdiocese. In the mid-1990s, approximately three hundred trees were harvested on its property. Some of the trees were giants; their rings dated their beginnings 130 years back to the Civil War. These trees were harvested in a way that did minimal damage to those remaining, and the lush appearance of the forest was left intact, to the credit of the camp's management and the logging company they hired. The loggers exhibited restraint and respect for the forest, leaving a healthy environment for the plants and animals that live there still and a beautiful environment where campers and visitors can enjoy a serene place to pitch a tent or take a walk or observe an owl. Logging and aesthetics need not be mutually exclusive, I've concluded.

With the help of people I respect, I'm gaining on my knee-jerk reaction to logging. In 2003, 120 nearby acres, some abutting my land, were logged. Some days the trees fell at the rate of one a minute, rumbling like thunder. I didn't like it, but I had begun to pay attention to trustworthy persons who assure me that a more diverse, healthy forest will be the result. Dr. George Parker, of the Purdue University School of Forestry, speaks about different types of forest management: clearcut, a management tool that sends shivers down the spines of some people, which gives shade-intolerant species the best chance to thrive; shelter wood, which removes many of the trees but leaves desirable species to re-seed the harvested area (the parent trees are harvested after desirable regeneration has occurred), allowing for the regeneration of a wide number of species; group selection, which creates one- to five-acre openings with emergent species then dependent upon the size of the opening; and single tree selection, the management system preferred by environmentalists and which favors shade-tolerant species.

Is it possible that some clearcuts are desirable? It depends on the desired future condition of the site, the habitat type the harvesting is occurring in, and the plant, animal, and natural communities being managed. Studies are being conducted to determine the forest management method most favorable for ruffed grouse, a bird species whose numbers are declining in some regions of our country, and other ground- or near-ground-nesting birds. The problem for these birds, according to an article in *National Wildlife* magazine, may be that forests are being allowed to grow, thus shading out understory vegetation. Following clearcuts, the herbaceous cover that grows up in newly sunny clearings provides protection for goldenwinged and chestnut-sided warblers and indigo buntings, as well as grouse. The article points out that prior to chainsaws, forest fires and other natural disturbances most likely maintained a mosaic of habitat types needed to sustain such a variety of species. The trick for land managers is to understand how the natural system works and which management tools need to be employed to maintain a viable natural system.

From what I've written, you may realize that I cherish trees. The place I've called home in Indianapolis since 1965 is under the arching branches of two American beech trees, perhaps as old as those I describe above. Their "arms" have grown to span most of my double lot, forming a giant cooling umbrella in the summer. In the winter their smooth bark offers an exquisite study in shades of gray. While I have grown to love my Brown County property, no two trees here can match the beauty of my urban trees.

Here in Brown County I have approximately nine forested acres that abut hundreds more. My woodland has a typical mix of deciduous trees, with American beech, maple, oak, hickory, sycamore, sassafras, and the ubiquitous early-succession tulip poplar. Black walnut, black cherry, black gum, black haw, pawpaw, persimmon, dogwood, and other species are scattered about. These trees nourish hundreds of species of invertebrates and vertebrates—myself included.

When I was a child, before fluoride was routinely added to our water systems, my teeth were barely through my gums when cavities developed. That's the way it is with our trees, in a sense. In spring, newly emerged leaves are riddled with holes. The difference between my teeth and spring leaves is that tooth cavities are bad and holey leaves are good. Why are holey leaves good? Because larvae eat the leaves, and birds thrive on larvae.

"Save the Rainforests" is a deserved and often heard plea. But how often do you hear the rallying cry "Save Indiana's Deciduous Forests"? After wintering in the tropical forests, dozens of bird species breed here or feed here on their way to northern boreal woods. *The Sibley Guide to Bird Life and Behavior* has helped me understand how important our forests are. Simply put, our mixed deciduous forests provide migratory stopover habitat, shelter for cavity-dwelling birds, and ample food resources and nesting habitat during the summer. Birds, like all life, strive to achieve high rates of reproductive success and survival. They need areas to "avail themselves of seasonally abundant food supplies, avoid the high density of nest predators and parasites found in the tropics, and take advantage of longer days for extended foraging," according to Sibley.

When we reduce the size of our forests, competition for food, nest sites, and mates increases and populations may decrease. Birds need territory and space, just as we do. Unfortunately, when people move into forests, many of us bring along our cats, a major predator of birds and other wildlife. Also, we inadvertently improve conditions for raccoons and opossums, predatory birds such as crows and blue jays, and brown-headed cowbirds, which are brood parasites. Nibbling off the edges of forests and clearing spaces within for homes and subdivisions creates a double whammy—more competition and more predators.

Warblers are representative of the numerous species that migrate to spend their summers in our woods. Their main food source comes from moth and butterfly larvae and other arthropods gleaned from leaves, twigs, and bark. They use grasses, leaves, bark, and other plant fibers for their nests, which they build in shrubs, trees, and cavities, and for domes (ovenbirds). They breed and rear their young here, then return in late summer to warm climates.

What is migration like? Sibley explains that it is seasonal and predictable. It happens annually, when the advantages from well-separated breeding and wintering grounds (i.e., Indiana and Costa Rica) are greater than the risks the journey poses in terms of energy and mortality. Bird migration is impressive and mysterious, whether it means long, nonstop flights over oceans, deserts, and mountains or a series of "hops" of 150 to 200 miles with stops in between to refuel for a few days. The non-soaring birds fly at night, when cooler temperatures allow the heat generated by flight to dissipate. Nighttime also tends to be calmer and allows birds to exert less energy. Soarers, such as the sandhill cranes that fly over Indiana in groups of hundreds during daylight, take advantage of thermals and upper winds and soar to their destinations.

Let's imagine migration for scarlet tanagers, a brilliantly feathered species that nests in Indiana. After wintering in Central America, they cross the Gulf of Mexico. Their over-water flight may take twelve hours, although in some years, when the winds are against them, it can take more than twenty-four hours. During bad crossings, they may stop to rest on offshore oil rigs, but many perish in the sea. Those that make it across are exhausted when they reach the Gulf shore of Louisiana, where they rest and refuel before flying back to the Indiana woods that they left seven months earlier.

When birds fly north in the spring, whether they stay here or stop temporarily, they need food en route. When they fly south in late summer, they need nectar, small fruits, and berries. When food becomes scarce in early fall, they depend upon the trees, shrubs, and vines that grow in our forests.

Sassafras berries are ambrosial food. High in lipids, they are vital to the health of living cells. Ripe in September, these blue-purple egg-shaped fruits sit in cherry-red cups supported by slender red stems. I once watched as a red-eyed vireo introduced its babe to these blue delicacies, the fledgling silently following its parent along a sassafras branch. For many languid September afternoon hours I watched birds feed in our sassafras grove. At one time in one tree there were pileated and red-bellied woodpeckers, summer and scarlet tanagers, nuthatches and thrushes; others times—

downy and hairy woodpeckers, flickers, chickadees, goldfinches, and more.

Sassafras fruit does not always develop. Freezing temperatures in May, on the heels of an early, warm spring, may zap tender new fruit. The seasons usually move along in orderly fashion, but in May 1996, when Joe and I stopped on our way back from Virginia, we were stunned to see that the leaves of tulip poplars, beeches, persimmons, hickories, redbuds, walnuts, and sumac were brown and crumpled, and our deck was littered with leaves. The cause was unseasonably low temperatures that had frozen the tender new growth on the tenth of May. Two weeks later, the trees were recovering and producing new green leaves, but the fruit was gone for that year.

Dogwoods produce shiny red fruit for the flocks of robins and thrushes that descend in mid-October. Milky-white bracts, the petal-like parts of our beloved flowering dogwoods, create heavenly clouds afloat in the early spring forests from the Midwest to the Atlantic Ocean. However, anthracnose has caused many dogwoods to die since the mid-1990s, or at best to produce twisted, rust-stained bracts with nearly barren branches. This has diminished both our visual pleasure and the amount of food available to birds.

Let's not overlook the value of mast, or nuts, from trees such as oaks, hickories, beeches, and walnuts, cherished by birds, squirrels, and deer.

Many Midwesterners love this part of the country because of the seasonal changes. After months of humid heat, the autumnal equinox arrives, and daytime highs usually reach only into the sixties. Sumac, sassafras, beech, and dogwood leaves turn red. Tulip

poplars release leaves that clatter down in a yellow and brown mini-
shower. October enters, invariably perfect those first days. By the
end of one October, oak trees lent the hills a soft, rounded look in
shades of deep mustard yellow, leathery brown, and ruby port red,
but that changed in a few hours. On a clear and calm but cold
morning, they let go in a gentle rain of leaves. Then the trees were
bare.

   Conservation is key to plant and wildlife viability. The American Bird Conservancy, working with a broad range of partner organizations and conservation scientists, has identified more than
five hundred sites in the U.S. that qualify for global *Important
Bird Area* status. (A map of these sites was printed in partnership
with the National Geographic Society in June 2002. Log on to
www.abcbirds.org for further information.) Brown County lies
within one of these sites. In connection with this, the Nature Conservancy has established the Brown County Hills Project in the
Brown County Hills Natural Region, covering more than three
hundred thousand acres in portions of seven counties. Research
into the national decline of forest interior migratory songbirds has
identified this area and two other Midwestern forests as critical
sources that attract migrating birds and that support successful
songbird breeding. These forests harbor a diverse array of plant
and animal species, including many that thrive in Indiana precisely
because this forest system is relatively intact and healthy. Cerulean
warblers, Louisiana waterthrushes, red-eyed vireos, Acadian fly-
catchers, yellow-billed cuckoos, and scarlet tanagers are species spe-
cifically cited. I believe that all of these, with the exception of the
cerulean warbler, nest on my property, or nearby. The assistance

that the Nature Conservancy offers, in partnership with public and private land owners, can teach us about good forest management, enlighten us about ways to conserve our land in perpetuity, and balance the effect of projected human growth against the ecological needs of the forest ecosystem. This is heartening news for our forests and their trees, and I'm glad that their office is in Nashville!

The issue of global warming is complex, but most who are concerned and who study the problem believe that maintaining healthy forests can slow the rate of warming. According to Tim Appenzeller in the February 2004 issue of *National Geographic*, each acre of a forest monitored in a recent study took roughly three-quarters of a metric ton of carbon out of the atmosphere annually. (The average American contributes more than five metric tons of carbon into the atmosphere a year; worldwide, humanity spews around eight billion metric tons annually.) Growing plants, through photosynthesis, remove a large percentage of the carbon dioxide gases (produced by our industrialized world in unprecedented quantities), use the carbon as an energy source and to build tissue, and release oxygen. Therefore, planting new forests on a grand scale is being encouraged, and preserving existing forests—and plant life in general—is seen as crucial. So again, let's hear it for "Save Indiana's Deciduous Forests!"

# Furry Creatures

The wilderness that was Indiana changed
apace. The seal of our great state depicts
an axeman felling a tree as a bison races
away from the rising sun.

By December 1816, when Indiana
entered statehood, bison were essentially
gone from the state.

—MARION T. JACKSON,
*The Natural Heritage of Indiana*

THOUGH NOT A MAMMAL, it is worth noting that the snapping
turtle occasionally seen in my pond descends from ancestral survivors of the collision between the asteroid and Earth sixty-five million years ago that caused the extinction of many animal species in
North America, including dinosaurs. Take a gigantic leap forward
to the end of the last ice age. After fourteen thousand years ago,
when the Clovis people migrated from Eurasia across the Bering
Strait and southward between the collapsing ice sheets in Canada,

large fauna such as the North American horse, camel, ground and giant sloth, sabertooth cat, lion, tapir, short-faced bear, and flat-headed peccary lived in North America. Over the next three or four thousand years, these animals, along with the mammoths, mastodons, and giant bison, began to go extinct. The scientific evidence is not clear whether this extinction was related to the arrival of humans in North America and the subsequent development of the Clovis point and overhunting by the Paleo-Indians, a response to dramatic climatic and environmental changes that were taking place as the planet developed interglacial conditions, or some combination of these factors.

The Ice Age was ending. Take a relatively short leap of ten thousand years or so into our own Holocene or Recent Age, arriving at the end of the eighteenth century, when this entire area was mature forest featuring oak-hickory on the uplands with some beech-maple areas in stream valleys. According to *Looking at History: Indiana's Hoosier National Forest Region, 1600 to 1950* by Ellen Sieber and Cheryl Ann Munson, wolf, elk, deer, bison, bear, cougar, beaver, squirrel, fox, raccoon, and rabbit were common. However,

> By the early 1800s beaver had been "trapped out," bison were very rare and cougar, wolf, bear, and elk were fast disappearing. . . . Deer and smaller mammals were important sources of food to pioneers, though deer eventually became over-hunted and could not reproduce. . . . An Englishman traveling through our region in the early 1820s described meeting two young men near the town of Hindostan, in Martin County.
>
> They had only been out two days; and not to mention a great number of turkeys, had killed sixteen deer and two bears, besides wounding several others. The bear is much more esteemed than the deer; first, because

his flesh sells at a higher price; and secondly, because his skin, if a fine large black one, is worth two or three dollars.

. . . Bear disappeared before 1850. Deer and wild turkey were gone or nearly absent in the state by the mid-to late 1890s.

In the early years of the twentieth century, poor soils hindered agricultural success, so many farmers had to rely on hunting and trapping to make a living. Meat and hides could provide a cash crop. Again, Sieber and Munson:

[L]imits were non-existent and sale of game was legal. In one season, grandpa killed over 1,500 rabbits; largest single day's haul was 68 rabbits, 4 quail, and 1 woodcock. . . . Fur-bearing animals were also plentiful. Grandpa kept hunting dogs for fox hunting by day or other fur-bearers at night. Raccoons, 'possums, skunks, mink, muskrats, weasels, foxes were taken by hunting or trapping. He had over 300 steel traps. He frequently hunted all night. He would designate a landmark several miles from home and tell [his sons] to meet him there at sunrise with the horses. He skinned animals while hunting to lessen weight in hunting coat or gunny sack.

They glide, leap, hop, tunnel, climb vertical walls, fly, and run— the mammals that share their home with me one hundred years later, at the beginning of the twenty-first century. They are chipmunks, coyotes, gray and fox squirrels, southern flying squirrels, foxes, moles, opossums, rabbits, raccoons, deer, bats, and mice. Some are a menace, particularly raccoons and deer. Distant coyotes howling and yipping in the night and early morning are thrilling.

I rarely see most animals that live around me, and I have never seen a live mole. However, the mounds I trip over and the tunnels I sink into let me know that the meadow supports a healthy colony of them. Since I don't attempt to nurture a lawn, we coexist. An entertaining article about moles appeared in the March 1994 issue of *Smithsonian:*

> Moles have "become an object of murderous indignation. People set traps designed to kill a mole by exploding a .32 blank cartridge in its face, by spearing it or by strangling it in a scissors grip. They put broken glass, razor blades, thorns, mothballs, and exhaust fumes down mole tunnels. They invest in sonic repelling devices, which use precisely the high-frequency sound waves that die out most rapidly in dirt, evoking indifference, if not scorn, among the moles. . . . A mole can dig 60 feet or more of subsurface tunnel in a day—roughly equivalent to a five-foot-tall woman burrowing the length of two football fields," while breathing carbon dioxide-laden air, the equivalent of what we exhale. Moles are insectivores and consume about half their weight daily. 15 or 20 nightcrawlers or grubs would whet their appetites. The genius of the tunnel system is that it brings the prey to the predator. Worms literally drop in. . . . all the mole has to do for a meal is amble periodically around its estate gathering up the latest crop of houseguests.

On the positive side, moles contribute to the soil by aerating it. Conversely, when they eat earthworms, the soil loses creatures that enrich it.

Eastern gray squirrels, the monkeys of our temperate forests, chatter and scold from their arboreal domain. Their blue-gray fur is tinted with tan patches; each hair of their fluffy tails is tipped with silvery white.

I've read multiple accounts of squirrels and the wily ways they use to reach bird feeders. In the summer of 2003, I incorrectly assumed that my configuration with a post-mounted baffle was sufficient. I was outside composing a late-June journal and noticed a gray squirrel approach the feeding area. It sprang upward four feet and bounced, like a well-directed billiard ball, off the two-and-a-half-foot cylindrical steel baffle, continuing onward and upward to the suspended platform feeder, which brimmed with sunflower seed. A stunning achievement! I immediately realigned the various feeders, to the squirrel's befuddlement. It spent hours analyzing the situation from several angles and tried its previous maneuver over and over, causing the entire arrangement to swing violently. Each time, it failed, arriving either at the peanut or the hummingbird feeder, neither of which gave sufficient purchase. I predicted that the squirrel would find a solution.

Before completing my journal, I recorded that I had guessed correctly. The squirrel made it all the way by bouncing off the baffle and scrabbling onto the hummingbird feeder long enough to grab the arm of the feeder, using it as a bridge to the platform. Outwitted, I made another trip to Wild Birds Unlimited for a separate post and arms from which to hang the sunflower seed feeder only. Baffling wildlife can be costly.

Generally, nature provides for our squirrelly friends. But until I learned from experience how hard black walnuts are to crack, gray squirrels and I competed for them. Squirrels can have them. Again and again they race for those pungent, fragrant orbs. They jump from branch to branch, tails curled and whipping the air for balance as they lunge from one tree to grab for another with branch tips smaller in diameter than a pencil. Then a headfirst run down a tree trunk, followed by a single leap to an uprooted tree stump to survey the situation and a few bounds gets the squirrel to a choice nut. From an elevated position on a rock or stump, it chews off the green husk and scampers off with the nut, still shrouded in its inky black layer. Twenty feet straight up, a run along its limbed highway, back to the ground, up and over the wood pile, twenty feet up another tree, across, down again, and out of sight. Later, from the squirrel's lofty perch, I hear its teeth scraping away the walnut's hard shell.

Gray and fox squirrels are ubiquitous throughout Indiana. Here, though, I have seen a fox squirrel one time only. Marion Jackson, editor of *The Natural Heritage of Indiana*, tells about a competitive squirrel hunt that took place in Bartholomew County, just east of Brown County, in 1834. Teams of fifty hunters each went out for a three-day period. The losing team was to host a squirrel barbecue for the winners. The winners brought in 900 squirrels; the losers had 783.

Chipmunks are very cute. I say that now that I've outwitted them, too, in some respects, and simply live with them in others. On average, three or four energetic juveniles emerge from their den in the spring, dashing about and chasing one another with their tails erect and joining a parent in search of food. (Later, they separate and become solitary.) Chipmunks, our small ground squirrels, have an uncanny ability to detect food intended for the birds. Within a few minutes after I put out seed in any number of places, they sense it and figure out how to get to it, climbing trees and board-and-batten siding and leaping chasms. Now the baffle stops them from reaching the feeders that hang from the arms above it. Seeds that fall to the ground provide an ample food supply as they fill their golden cheeks, bulging with as much as a full tablespoon of sunflower seeds (or even four small acorns) in each, and race back to their underground storage place to stash their booty.

Raccoons are agile and intelligent, with dexterous front paws and extraordinary climbing ability. They survive too well and are overly abundant. They are significant predators of nesting birds. Vexatious and exasperating, they tear apart bird feeders for seed and unscrew the caps of hummingbird feeders to chug-a-lug the syrup. But again, I have learned to work around them. Raccoon baffles on pole-mounted feeders prevent these nocturnal scavengers from reaching the goodies. Attractive nuisances such as hummingbird feeders come inside at night.

Southern flying squirrels are the most endearing of the neighboring mammals. They make faint squeaky, twittering chirps at night. When I first heard them, I thought they were migrating birds resting in the surrounding trees. Eventually I connected those timid sounds to the squirrels that found seed in the bird feeder hanging from a pulley fastened to a tulip poplar branch. (I admit to having a bias in favor of flying squirrels over others in the squirrel family.) With one on board, I slowly lowered the feeder so that we could eye each other closely. I touched its whiskers and it "flew" to the ground, then scurried away through a carpet of white violets beneath the chestnut oak. Their furry, flat tails act like the stabilizing feathers, the vanes, on an arrow when they leap and glide (not fly) with the loose flaps of skin stretched taut between their wrists and their ankles. Only five to six inches long, they have disproportionately large, mouse-like eyes and large ears that alert them to nighttime predators. Their scientific name is *Glaucomys volans*—"gray mouse that flies."

Anne and Tom Petersen, former Broad Ripple neighbors, stayed with me one October night. While sipping morning coffee, we heard and then saw an agitated Carolina wren near the birdhouse nailed to a hickory tree. Tom exclaimed, "There's somebody in there," referring to the face inside the opening. A furry head with bulging eyes peered out—a flying squirrel. Other birds joined the wren—titmice, chickadees, a downy woodpecker, and a yellow-rumped warbler. The frenzy soon subsided, and the nocturnal squirrel resumed its daytime slumber.

When I was in grade school, Mr. and Mrs. Campbell showed movies of the wild animals they befriended and fed at their Michigan home. Salt and Pepper were skunks that came to eat within a few feet of them. I wanted to be like the Campbells when I grew up and be close to wild animals. More than half a century later, my mind's eye brings those idyllic images back. Those simple movies, with charming scenes of man and animals at ease with one another, contributed to my deep infatuation with the natural world.

# Smitten with Bugs

WE HUMANS ARE LIVING THINGS, although not fungi, bacteria, protists, or plants. We have spines and interior skeletons. We are vertebrate animals, or chordates, along with birds, reptiles, amphibians, fish, and others. Arthropods constitute the other main phylum within the animal kingdom. Look yourself over: If you have jointed legs, a hard outer exoskeleton, and no backbone, you're an arthropod! You might be a cone-headed katydid, one of 1.5 million species of arthropods that range from microscopic springtails crawling in the soil to giant crabs with legs a yard long. Arthropods comprise up to ninety percent of all animal species.

Here in Brown County, I watched orange and brown butterflies savor hoary mountain mint. Jet black and iridescent green damselflies and dragonflies darted around the pond. Hidden insects hummed and buzzed nonstop in the meadow. Joe spotted the first walkingstick either of us had seen in years. I soon realized that insects, a class of arthropods, deserve our attention along with the birds, amphibians, and flowers that I admired.

"Bug" is an untechnical term "used by entomologists when they are being informal to mean all those little animals that creep, jump and fly about, including insects, but also spiders, daddy longlegs, ticks and mites, in the class Arachnida, as well as the terrestrial order Isopoda, the sow bugs, and centipedes and millipedes, too," according to Sue Hubbell in *Broadsides from the Other Orders: A Book of Bugs*. She writes:

> Differentness is what made me fall in love with bugs. . . . The day I became an entomophile I was studying insect circulatory systems. The insect body, I read, is filled with hemolymph, free and unconstrained by vessels or arteries, except for a single long one that runs along the insect's back or dorsum. The business part of this vessel is called a heart. . . . Their way seemed to me to be elegant and efficient. I knew it had been working well for hundreds of millions of years. I was hooked. I wanted to know everything about bugs and how they had managed to survive so successfully.

Bugs are vital to nature's food chain. Personally, I find winged bugs the most interesting—butterflies, moths, bees, wasps, grasshoppers, mantises, cicadas, and water striders. They sting, spread disease, bore holes in wood, and destroy crops; they pollinate, beautify, intrigue, and amaze.

If I had elected biology rather than chemistry to fulfill my high school's science requirement, I would have studied insects, all of which have six legs and three body regions—head, thorax, and abdomen. I would have learned that the scientific names of winged insects have two parts—the first, or prefix, describing the type of wing, and the second, *-ptera*, from the Greek word for wing.

Moths, butterflies, and skippers have wings with tiny scales. They are Lepidoptera. Joe and I walked up a summer's dry creek bed and met two teenage boys carrying BB guns. They reminded us that we had met them earlier that spring near the same place in the valley. I remembered them romping and swinging on grapevines. I hoped that I came across as conversational and not accusatory when I asked what they did with their guns. "We just shoot butterflies and things, not birds," they responded. "Not on our place," I warned. Then I recalled my friend's warning—"Don't alienate idle kids"—as Joe defused the scene with a discussion of gun models.

In contrast to shooting butterflies "for fun" is gardening *for* butterflies. Butterfly gardening is widely desirable and popular, but success depends upon the presence of larval food. You can plant all the nectar-producing flowers in the world, but without the correct host plant on which they can lay their eggs, you won't have butterflies. The tiny caterpillars that hatch from those eggs must have the larval food they've evolved with through time. For example, the caterpillars of spicebush swallowtails need to eat the leaves of spicebush shrubs and sassafras trees.

Caterpillars of Lepidoptera are fantastic. They may be smooth or bumpy, with or without knobs, hairy or hairy with tufts or pencils and with or without a rear horn, slug-like, bristled or with branched spines. My favorite is the cecropia caterpillar. It is smooth, green, and dotted with blue, yellow, and red knobs or tubercles. Most butterflies and moths are beneficial, so forgive their larvae if they eat your plants. That is how they survive. In mid-May, however, eastern tent caterpillars, not to be confused with the gypsy moth caterpillar, are often abundant, and to some they are definitely disgusting. They can defoliate an entire black cherry tree. Carried by wind or merely dropping from above, they may be found on railings, decks, outside walls, the ground, everywhere. They squirt when they're accidentally stepped on.

Among the most stunning adults of the Lepidoptera order are giant silkworm moths. Over more than a decade here, I have seen four silkworm moth species. In 1992, at dusk, a luna moth appeared. I had not seen one since my childhood. Another beat its wings and tapped its feet against the window near my reading lamp. Its fervent, futile attraction to the light was unnerving, so I switched off the lamp and went to bed.

Midsummer 1997, two silkworm moths were drawn to our lights. First came a male io. I had photographed an io caterpillar but had never seen its adult form. It was furry with wings the color of whipped egg yolks and had muted lavender dots on the forewings. With its wings open, giant eyes on its hind wings stared back at me. A polyphemus fluttered at the lamp-lit window the next night.

A mixed flock of small birds made a ruckus twenty feet high in the tulip poplar. Snakes cause similar fracases. Would a snake be that high? Chickadees, titmice, and gnatcatchers flitted from branch to branch, fussing and chattering. With binoculars I saw a dark brown triangular form with wide, paler margins undulating along the inner edge. I could not see eyespots, but I deduced that a cecropia moth, the fourth species of silkworm, clung to the underside of a branch. Had that motionless, harmless creature alarmed that mob of birds? A robin flew in, took a look, and left. Big deal.

Why aren't giant silkworm moths as common in Brown County now as I remember them in Indianapolis fifty years ago? Their larvae feed on the foliage of a broad range of deciduous trees, yet I may not see one during an entire summer.* I compare this to Gene Stratton-Porter's experience more than a hundred years ago in northeastern Indiana, which she described in "Tales You Won't Believe":

> This was a month [May] during which I scarcely slept. Each night when I went to bed, I looked over my collection (chrysalises) and listened with cocoons held to my ear as one would hold a watch. If I heard struggling and efforts of emergence going inside the cocoon I laid it on a tray beside my pillow in order that I might be awake and ready to make my records when the moths appeared. . . . About two o'clock in the morning I was awakened by sounds that I did not understand. There was a faint vibration in the air, a soft bumping against the screen on the outside, a metallic sound as if the feet of dozens of moths were walking over the copper screen.
>
> I threw back the sheet and went to the door. . . . there were uncountable numbers of Cecropia moths. . . .
>
> As I lifted this moth from the screen, she showered me [with a fine spray], over my shoulders, over my night-dress, even to my bare feet. I knew by experience when I had her on my fingers that flight was impossible to her owing to her weight and the lack of exercise of her new wings. First I placed her on a window beside the door; then feeling sure, I took her on my fingers, swung open the door, and advanced to the steps. Stand-

---

* According to the Xerces Society, many entomologists blame the decline on parasitoids that were introduced to control gypsy moths—sadly, an unsuccessful venture.

ing there, between the bloom-whitened apple trees on either side, in the full radiance of the moonlight . . . with my shoulders and nightgown wet with spray, I became the best moth bait that the world knows and the night became a vibrant thing, a thing of velvet wings. . . . the moths . . . alighted on my head, on my shoulders, on my hands; they clung to my night robe; they walked over my feet; they flocked over the apple trees; they fluttered through the moonlight; and there was no one to see or to know the poignant beauty of that perfect May hour.

I lack both the expertise and the accumulated knowledge to put my observations into perspective as Porter did. What is the benchmark? Take the case of great spangled fritillaries as an example. One Fourth of July, a single great spangled fritillary gathered nectar from sumac blossoms. The previous year, in contrast, dozens had gathered at the same sumacs as well as on purple coneflowers and butterfly weeds. The perspective of *Butterfly Gardening* by the Xerces Society comforts me somewhat. People claim to see dozens of butterflies around a particular plant in their gardens, but this is unlikely to happen every day, or even every year, they write. They don't say why beyond "random chance." What is the explanation when they are in small numbers? A too-frigid winter? A May freeze? Heat and drought in June? Massive use of pesticides? Absence of larval food the previous year? All of these or none?

Monarch butterflies are rarely seen here, with one exception. It was August 15, 1993. The sky was cloudy, and strong winds blew from the north. I first saw one monarch. Then, looking up through binoculars, I discovered a sky peppered with them. They flew southwesterly in a wave that lasted forty-five minutes. Another day, a monarch narrowly averted becoming a phoebe's lunch. The butterfly's

loopy path took it over the far flower bed, back to the near one,
past the deck, across the lower patio, over the stone wall, and into
the woods, where suddenly a phoebe darted after it, lunged, and
made contact. The unusual butterfly escaped.

July's wild tiger lilies are ambrosia to tiger and spicebush swallowtails. One swallowtail, approaching a lily, was the missed target
of a hungry crow. Occasionally, both black and yellow swallowtails
flutter at the same bright-orange deep-throated flower, only to be
challenged by a hummingbird. When these showy swallowtails, the
size of small birds, drift by within an arm's length, they carry me to
another realm.

Vladimir Nabokov was a literary genius as well as a renowned
lepidopterist and the first to identify the Karner blue butterfly as a
distinct subspecies. In a lecture at Cornell University during the
1950s, he said: "The pupa splits as the caterpillar had split—it is
really a last glorified moult, and the butterfly creeps out—and in
its turn hangs down from the twig to dry. She is not handsome at
first. She is very damp and bedraggled. But those limp implements
of hers that she has disengaged, gradually dry, distend, the veins
branch and harden—and in twenty minutes or so she is ready to
fly. . . . You will ask—what is the feeling of hatching? Oh, no doubt,
there is a rush of panic to the head, a thrill of breathless and strange
sensation, but then the eyes see, in a flow of sunshine, the butterfly
sees the world, the large and awful face of the gaping entomologist."

Beetles, such as fireflies and weevils, have sheath-like, armored,
horny, or leathery wings and are members of the order Coleoptera.

For those of us who live east of the Rocky Mountains, summer and fireflies, or lightning bugs, are synonymous. Most of us, urban and rural alike, at some point in our lives have chased a firefly and cupped it momentarily in our hands. Many have filled a jar with them before releasing them to the night air. In vast numbers, they can light your way in the darkness, as they did when Joe and I ambled along Wallow Hollow one June night. We melded into a silent spectacle of thousands of flickering points of light, a fanciful world of fairies with firefly lanterns like those in a framed print that hung by my bed when I was a child.

There are 136 species of fireflies in North America, members of the family Lampyridae. I learned from Peterson's field guide to beetles that all larvae and most adults produce light. The process is chemical and nearly a hundred percent efficient, with almost no energy given off as heat; even the eggs of some species glow faintly. Most male fireflies flash in flight and are then attracted to answering flashes of the female on the ground. Each species has a characteristic and sometimes even distinctive pattern of flashes. Depending on the location and the time of year, a student of fireflies can recognize most species solely by the number and duration of flashes and the interval between them. Some females answer the flashes of males of other species, then subdue and eat any male that is attracted to them; this is termed aggressive mimicry. One mid-May night I discerned two distinct species. One flew horizontally a few feet above the ground, flashed a yellow-orange light three or four times rapidly, and drifted until the next series three or four seconds later. Another flew high up in the trees and flashed a single, prolonged greenish light while either ascending or descending.

According to an article in *National Wildlife*, scientists at Tufts

University, using computer-generated lights, tested flash patterns exhibited by various species to determine which ones attracted the most females. Females responded best to longer flashes. The scientists suspected that the longer flash might be correlated with a larger spermatophore, "the high-protein nutritional gift a male firefly gives a female after mating, which she uses to feed her eggs." Indeed, that proved to be true. Co-author Christopher Cratsley writes, "Males have only about ten opportunities to mate, so they need to stand out in the frenzied crowd of competitors and communicate to females that they're worthy of consideration."

Lady beetles, known widely as "ladybugs," are in the order Coleoptera. Like fireflies, they are endearing creatures. With their orange-red wings and black dots, they are a favorite subject of artists and toy makers. And many of us remember the distressing rhyme: "Ladybug, Ladybug, fly away home. Your house is on fire. Your children are burning."

Lady beetles' charisma and beneficial properties make them an attractive flagship species, in the words of Cornell University entomologists Erin Stephens and John Losey. Forty of our fifty states have named official state insects (Indiana may consider the Say's firefly as its state insect during the 2004 Legislature), and five of these are lady beetles. Unfortunately, the nine-spotted species (*Coccinella novemnotats*, abbreviated to C-9), designated by New York because it was the most common of lady beetle species, is now "endangered" there and "threatened" nationally. Their decline, as well as that of others in the coccinellid family, naturally raises questions: Why has a once common species of a very common insect family declined precipitously, and how can the same fate be avoided for other native coccinellids? Habitat alteration is a prime suspect, but many suggest that introduced species, those that overwinter by the hundreds and thousands in some of our homes and garages, have played a role. Lady beetles are important predators in both natural and agricultural systems, preying upon aphids, scales, and other soft-bodied insects; thus we must understand their needs and work to preserve them. The Xerces Society, www.xerces.org, dedicated to protecting the diversity of life through the conservation of invertebrates, can provide further information. When I see lady beetles in the future, I will count their spots, looking for the two, nine, and thirteen spots of native species. Seven spots? I will recognize the creature as one of those that threaten my sense of well-being when they swarm around me in Alfred Hitchcock-esque numbers.

Black weevils are beetles that lay eggs at the base of purple coneflowers, prairie dock, and cup plant in my meadow. There must be some ingenious reason why the weevil nearly severs the hollow stem beneath the blossom, leaving a tiny portion that acts like a hinge, before laying its eggs. The blossom falls downward and wilts, yet remains loosely attached to the stem. The eggs later hatch into tiny larvae inside the wilted flower and feed there. Hundreds of flowers have been nipped in the bud, so to speak. Stinkbugs exhibit somewhat similar behavior, sucking fluids or juices from plant stems four to five inches below the flower buds, which then wilt and die. Stinkbugs sense my predator's approach and often drop to the ground and disappear before I can make contact. Their "stink," by the way, is like the fragrance of almonds—quite pleasant.

Flies, mosquitoes, midges, and gnats have two wings and are in the order Diptera.

I'm surprised that flies are generally in small numbers around my property and are not noteworthy, beyond the fact that there may be ninety thousand species worldwide. Mosquitoes are in small numbers also, most summers, and are generally tolerable. The exception was the unusually wet summer of 2003. Since the mosquito-borne disease called the West Nile virus entered the United States in the late 1990s, most of us have been forced to rethink our tolerance for these creatures. This virus can be fatal to humans and other animals.

Water boatmen, water striders, bedbugs, and ambush bugs are in the order Hemiptera. The name comes from the fact that their anterior wings are half leathery and half membranous.

The word "tattoo" may call to mind a design on our skin or the repetitive drumming of a woodpecker on a hollow branch, but it is also a seductive set of wavelets sent by male water striders across the thin surface film upon which they live to attract females. Water striders are relatively common on my pond and on Cassie Creek. The ones I've watched appear to be wingless, but some are born with wings and some without, a phenomenon called alary polymorphism by scientists. The winged ones colonize new puddles and ponds, and even temporary ones such as chuckholes and ruts.

Wasps, ants, and bees have membranous wings and belong to the order Hymenoptera.

A yellow jacket once flew into my dessert dish, which was sitting on the outside table. It wallowed in the slurry of chocolate syrup and melted vanilla ice cream, then came to a dead halt, smothered in chocolate ecstasy. I dipped it out and placed it into the birdbath, where, if still alive, it could cleanse itself of the sticky coating. Within a few minutes it swam, and in another few minutes it stood on the high, dry rim, preening its antennae. Then off it went.

Yellow jackets are small wasps (not bees, as is commonly believed) that nest in the ground. Away from the nest they are generally nonthreatening, but if their nests are inadvertently disturbed, for instance when we mow the grass, they become a swarm of aggressive attackers. A wasp is any of numerous social or solitary insects, having a slender body with a constricted abdomen, two pairs of membranous wings, and a mouth adapted for biting; the females have an ovipositor, often modified as a sting. Those bald-faced creatures that build football-sized aerial nests made of macerated wood pulp in trees are hornets—large, stinging social wasps. Bees? Check it out.

A thread-waisted wasp floundered in the birdbath, where it had come for a sip of water. I lifted it out. Afterwards it spent an hour in recovery, practicing calisthenics, it seemed—balancing first on two legs and then on its mandibles, curving its abdomen up, then horizontally, then down, and preening its antennae, legs, and wings.

Paper wasps hibernate in the cabin's crevices during winter. When we heat the cabin, they occasionally emerge. Dazed, they drag themselves across the carpeted floor or manage to fly but bump into the window. They relish the ripe banana occasionally offered. If you can catch them in a lethargic state and engrossed in eating, examine these handsome insects with their compound eye segments and the

three jet-black single-lens eyes atop their heads. Beware, though—
when they nest, they too are aggressive. I have been targeted more
than once.

Respectfully, I once observed paper wasp behavior in a small
hive from a few inches away. (I thought I had captured the following scenario on film, only to later discover an empty camera. Fortunately I had sketched the cells and recorded the events on paper.)
Joe accidentally knocked a paper wasp nest loose from under the
deck rail. He placed it on the rail, now stem side down and cell
openings up. Despite the disruption, I had the rare opportunity to
observe their lives for three days. There were forty-nine cells; twenty-
eight were covered with a white, paper-like cap. The creatures worked
day and night. They would rest, then stir, tend the hive, peer into
cells, and enter some that appeared empty. A wasp alighted two
feet from the hive with a one-quarter-inch pale green ball, kneaded
from the regurgitated solid parts of caterpillars, an excellent protein source. At the hive three workers greeted it. One accepted the
morsel. It ate part, perhaps half, while the others watched guard-
edly. Then it removed a fragment, entered a chamber, left the piece,
and backed out, repeating this procedure until the morsel was gone.

Midafternoon of the second day, a wasp ate or pulled away part
of the cap from a covered cell, exposing an eye, the "beak," and an
antenna of what appeared to be a fully formed wasp. After removing more cap, the worker pulled and pulled on a leg. Finally the
whole cell was uncovered and the whole head revealed. There was
no sign of life. In the meantime, a worker went headfirst into another cell, pulled out a pale yellow blob, and flew away with it,

colliding with the Deer-X fencing. The blob stuck to the plastic net. I plucked it off and brought it back to the nest. In less than a minute a wasp came, consumed it, regurgitated the yellow mass, and fed it to three of the four active larvae (white blobs with gray mouthparts). The larval mouthparts moved and worked the yellow mass until it was consumed. Through the next day, I made notes about the cells—which larvae looked alive, which desiccated; which were active, which quiet. One, with the form of its wings evident, was carried away, and not returned. Life in the little nest was not thriving. I hoped to continue my observations, so three adults and their nest went to Indianapolis. I left them in a jar on the patio table—only to soon see a squirrel jump onto the table, go nose down into the jar, and devour the nest.

I was sitting on the pier when I first heard and then saw some insects digging holes in the sandy beach by the pond. They had black and orange striped abdomens and shiny, burnt orange colored wings held lengthwise along their backs. Dozens, working singly that midsummer afternoon, sent grains of sand flying into the air as they dug, some grains landing three and four inches away. A year later I learned that they were sand wasps.

Some might accuse me of being remiss if I don't mention ants. Ants are so common that I overlook them. For most of the summer of 2003, however, I could not help but notice them and their relationship with a tulip poplar tree. Streams of ants traveled approximately twenty-five feet from a location beneath the ground by the cabin near my bedroom, across the lawn (this path, over time, created a one-inch-by-one-half-inch trench littered with plant debris on each side), eight feet up the tree trunk to two branches and out to the ends, perhaps another fifteen or twenty feet, to scales, insects that produce a waxy covering that resembles marine barnacles. There was sticky goo under the shell. Were the ants harvesting this?

Dragonflies and damselflies are tooth-jawed and belong to the order Odonata. Unlike the previous species mentioned, the scientific name for this order refers to mouthparts, not wings. This is the single carryover from the classification system devised by Johann Christian Fabricius, an eighteenth-century Danish entomologist. There is a distinct difference between dragonflies and damselflies. Dragonflies hold their wings horizontally when resting, and damselflies hold their wings upright and together. Interestingly, there are societies devoted to Odonata, and there are individuals who maintain Odonata life lists just as some of us maintain bird lists.

Because I see dragonflies frequently in and above my meadow, it would be easy to make the mistake of not associating them with their aquatic life. Several rest daily on the upright seed heads of English plantain or hunt prey in the air above. Dozens zoom back and forth above the meadow like toy helicopters, making sharp U-turns at the fence line. Remarkably swift, dragonflies have been clocked flying 35—some say up to 60!—miles per hour. Add equally remarkable visual acumen to that speed, and you have a formidable foe—with wraparound eyes that extend their field of vision to nearly 360 degrees, and up to 12,000 simple eyes in each compound one.

In actuality, most of a dragonfly's life—from one to four years, depending on the species—is spent crawling or swimming underwater as a predatory larva. It splits and sheds its skin seven to fourteen times as it grows. It then climbs out of the water to shed one last time and, in a seemingly magical transformation, emerges moments later as a mature dragonfly. I arrived at the pond one September day soon after such a moment. A rustling sound came from across the pond, where a Swainson's thrush was eating a piece of cellophane, I thought. Actually, the thrush was consuming a small dragonfly with cellophane-like wings, akin to one I'd just found that had split its final exoskeleton. (Many split exoskeletons were floating on the pond that day.)

In both the underwater nymph stage and the adult stage, dragonflies are voracious feeders and snatch prey in a dragon-like way. Adult dragonflies catch their prey on the wing, and their maxillae serve as meat forks, holding a captive so that it can be carved into convenient portions by the mandibles of the upper jaw.

Cockroaches, mantises, grasshoppers, crickets, and sticks have wings that are straight and narrow and are in the order Orthoptera.

It was a fresh and breezy Fourth of July night. Distant lightning flashed as Joe and I sat on our patio wall, sipping Australian port. Beyond our wildflower garden, we noticed a faint, stationary luminescent flicker and found an unidentifiable pale-green insect trapped in a spider's web on the fence. There were many other insects on the fence, mostly grasshopper instars tinted pink, green, and white, feeling their way with arching antennae much longer than their tiny bodies.

Instars are the intermediary stage between the egg and the mature adult of insects. The process is called simple metamorphosis. They molt their exoskeleton several times and may closely resemble the adult form between molts. (In contrast, butterflies and moths develop through complete metamorphosis.) One unidentified instar, the shape of a grasshopper only many times smaller, looks like an exquisite piece of gold jewelry inlaid with bands of turquoise enamel.

Crickets and grasshoppers bring summer nights alive with their throbbing calls. We hear them but don't often see them because they are superbly camouflaged. Katydids, for example, have a remarkable resemblance to green leaves.

Katydids, one of several species of long-horned grasshoppers, call as early as mid-July and continue into November some years. True katydids are those that repeat the familiar "Katy did; Katy didn't." They differ from arboreal katydids, which inhabit upper elevations in trees, and bush or angular-winged katydids. Bush katydids are the ones that make me jump when, clinging to window and door screens, they suddenly blurt out their high-pitched tropical rattles. To make their sounds, katydids raise their forewings and scrape the rigid edge of the right forewing near its attachment to the thorax against teeth on the file vein on the underside of the other wing. Scrape scrape. Scrape scrape.

A gauzy cloud veiled the stars of the Milky Way that we had walked up our meadow path to see, so our attention turned toward the insects making rasping buzzes on and off every second. Before it retreated and became as one with a blade of grass, we saw an elegant leaf-green katydid.

Late in the evening of October 29, 1996, the temperature was a relatively warm 69 degrees. Hundreds of insects speckled the outside of the window near the reading lamp. Katydids grazed the glass like cows grazing grass—slowly, contentedly munching their way along, perhaps, as Joe suggested, feeding on pollen or the aeolian plankton referred to by Edward. O. Wilson in *The Diversity of Life*. Most orthopterans are plant eaters, but that night a predaceous katydid, with difficulty, ate a small insect.

Two walkingsticks chose the front screen door for their trysting place one early October morning. The male was a rich brown color and twig-like with green legs; the female was longer, wider, and lighter in color. For five hours they barely moved while his two front legs held her head, his middle pair gripped her thorax, and his third pair held on to the screen. His clasper grasped her tail end with his genitalia arched beneath and entering hers. We went in and out through other doors that morning.

While I was reading outdoors one day, a walkingstick dropped onto my book. The odd but superbly designed creature climbed onto my extended hand. I covered it with my other hand and let it go on the wooden rail near the straight-sided pot used as a crude device to measure rainfall. The stick quickly walked to the pan, went up and onto the underside of the handle, and deliberately assumed its "I'm really a twig" posture.

I close this treatise on Brown County bugs and hope that you who read it join me as a fellow entomophile.

# Frogs, Toads, and Tadpoles—
# Oh My!

$A$s Brown County is my spawning ground and the biological soup I dip into, savor, explore, and digest, my pond is the spawning arena for seven species of frogs.

On April 12, 1991, suggestive, vibrating sounds came from the pond. Male American toads were calling for mates. They continued through that night and the next day, singing in unison as though following a musical director. G-F♯-G-G♯-G—each note held five or six seconds. Joe and I were astonished when we arrived at the pond and found a toad orgy in progress. There were hundreds of toads, alone and in twos, threes, and fours. The color of their skin

172 Swimming with Frogs

varied—pale yellow-green, buff, rust, and dark green with black spots. They swam, embraced, attacked, kicked, and rolled and roiled the surface of the pond. Gelatinous, spiraling strands of ten thousand eggs and more, black on one side and white on the other, were tangled amid underwater vegetation. The females were producing more strands while in the copulatory embrace called amplexus with males fertilizing their eggs. A day later the pond was quiet, the toads gone, their tumultuous breeding season ended. But my deep interest in frogs had begun.

I was still a struggling novice two years later, ignorant and confused. Was the pulsating chorus I heard that of spring peepers or another species? Could the sound I heard be described more like a fingernail running along the small teeth of a comb, a thumb rubbing against a balloon, or a sheep with a cold? I needed a recording of frog calls so that I could compare the differences and match calls to species. Since many frogs are active at night and are rarely seen, sound is all you can go by. And if you can't see them, how can a guidebook of pictures help? I had to learn the calls. Then I read about "Voices of the Night: The Calls of the Frogs and Toads of Eastern North America," a tape produced in 1982 through the Library of Natural Sounds, Cornell Laboratory of Ornithology. I ordered a copy.* Listening to it the first time, I turned the proverbial corner when I played recorded calls simultaneously with live ones and compared them. Cope's gray treefrogs were my first test. After matching recorded with actual calls, I went to the pond twice with a guidebook and a flashlight. The second time, I was elated

---

*Today several websites offer sounds of nature, including frogs.

when I found a frog and verified its identification. The same year I received helpful written material from the Nature Conservancy and an instructional tape, "The Wisconsin Frogs."

Variation of calls within individual species helps a female frog judge the male with which she will choose to mate. Some females prefer males with deeper calls, while others prefer those that call more frequently or for longer periods of time, indicating that they are stronger and have extra energy to burn. Size may be another winning attribute for a male, an indication that he feeds well, digests food well, has few parasites, and has a good immune system.

Toads and frogs are of the same order, Anura (from New Latin and Greek for "no tail"). Adults lack tails, and they have well-developed forelimbs and even larger hind legs. Their heads seem to be attached directly to their bodies. They have a voice to attract mates, drive off intruders, and signal distress and presence. All are carnivorous. Most are prone to desiccation and are therefore confined to wet or moist habitats and return to water to breed. The fertilized eggs hatch into tadpoles, which later transform into young frogs and toads.

True frogs, including the well-known bullfrog, have smooth, wet skin with slim waists, long legs, pointed toes, and extensive webbing on the hind feet. They are excellent jumpers. Adults are truly amphibious, typically living along the edge of water and entering it daily to catch prey, to flee danger, or to mate.

Toads are squat and plump with dry, rough, warty skin. Lacking the long posterior legs that allow true frogs to leap away quickly from predators, toads have parotoid glands from which they can secrete a foul-tasting fluid to deter predators. Fowler's and American toads spend time around the cabin in the summer. Normally I see them outside, but once, to my surprise, I found a toad backed up against the base of my kitchen cabinets. Another peered at me from a narrow space in a stone wall, allowing me to see only its bulging button eyes with 24K-gold lids.

A young toad sheds its skin every few weeks; an adult dispenses with its skin four times a year. The skin splits, then the toad uses its front feet to pull the old skin off, gradually stuffs the castoff suit into its mouth, and finally swallows the whole affair. This takes around five minutes.

According to AmphibiaWeb (www.amphibiaweb.org), in 2002 there were 4,718 species of frogs and toads worldwide and 101 in the United States. The range and habitat descriptions of the 17 species listed as living in Indiana suggest that 9 should find my pond a suitable breeding site—the wood frog, the spring peeper, the chorus frog, the American toad, Cope's gray treefrog (and possibly the eastern gray treefrog), the green frog, the bullfrog, Fowler's toad, and possibly the southern leopard frog. Most have.

The late Dr. Sherman Minton, author of *Amphibians & Reptiles of Indiana,* was a friend of ours and a former colleague of Joe's. He was also a world-renowned herpetologist, a specialist in the branch of zoology concerned with reptiles (snakes and lizards, crocodilians, turtles, loricates, and tuataras) and amphibians* (frogs and toads, salamanders and newts, and caecilians). Sherm was part of my bag of tools, along with tape recordings, a flashlight, and guidebooks.

---

*The word "amphibian" comes from Greek *amphibios,* meaning "dual life": tadpoles live in water, while adults are land-dwelling.

When April 23, 1993, came and went with no sign of American toad eggs, he was reassuring. He said that conditions differ from one year to the next. Three days later, a toad headed in the direction of the pond. Three days after that, more began to congregate, and that night, at least a hundred or more were swimming or floating spread-eagled—mini skinny dippers. Their eyes, just above the water's surface, shone yellow in the flashlight beam. Heading up the path, I glanced back at them. Planet Venus cast a shimmering white streak across the pond as the toads called erotically for mates. The next day, the action was furious. When not mating, the males sat on cattail islands and other floating plant debris and called, their throats ballooning out in song. The frenzy subsided in twenty-four hours, leaving behind a dead toad tangled amid the debris in the murky water and a lifeless, pale female locked in amplexus with two males. Their numbers dropped in 1994 to a small fraction of previous years. Nonetheless, they returned, with spring peepers adding their sleigh bell calls to the chorus.

February days here can be spring-like and warm. A spring peeper calls as if to say, "Hey, anybody else out yet?" Sometimes another answers. It was 62 degrees at 8:30 and raining on one of those February evenings when a spring peeper appeared on the window. Outside, we held a flashlight near the frog. It was pink, about an inch long, with a pointed head like a salamander's and with the telltale cross on its back. It put its feet on the lens of the flashlight and stared into the bulb. Then it jumped to my hand, to Joe's, back to mine, and then back to the window. Inside again, we examined the frog's belly. It made me think of a rock's-eye view of a rock climber, clinging to hard stone with arms and legs outspread.

On a night when a comet and stars were reflected on the pond, I tried to find a spring peeper. The cacophony from multitudes of peepers was torturous, and I held my hands over my ears. Amid that racket, I could find only a single peeper, which grasped a tiny sapling.

Frog breeding begins in early spring. The timing is dependent upon water temperature. The earliest breeders, wood frogs, chorus frogs, and spring peepers, require the water to be at least 50 degrees Fahrenheit. American toads require 60 degrees. The eggs and egg agglomerations of the various species differ significantly from one another: "Tiny, black in filmy egg mass. Initially floats. One inch in diameter." "Attached singly or in small groups to underwater plants." "Globular mass attached to stems." "Light colored, gray above, white below. In a film. Hatch 2–5 days." Most often I miss the spawn. When I do see spawn, it can be difficult to connect the egg mass to a specific species. The long spirals of American toad and Fowler toad eggs are a distinct exception. Common literature lacks sufficient information.

When the water temperature rises to 70 degrees or more, usually in May, American toad eggs have hatched and other frog species breed. A green frog octet calls with sounds like plucked loose banjo strings. Their calls consist of a single plunk or two or three descending plunks, repeated after a one-second break. Because their tones vary, you can differentiate among them. Each takes a turn, rarely overlapping. During daylight, you can see their bulging canary-yellow throats when they call.

Once I saw tadpoles darting into the strands of a milky, gelatinous egg mass and pulling at it with their mouths. Curious about this behavior, I called a U.S. Fish and Wildlife biologist. Would tadpoles of one species predate the egg cases of another? The biologist said that egg cases are rich in protein and newly emerged tadpoles eat their cases, but he wasn't familiar with the situation I described. I hoped that he could identify the eggs, tiny like the period at the end of this sentence. Examined with a strong magnifying lens, they were shaped like rice grains and were tan, slightly mottled. He turned for help to *Amphibians and Reptiles of Missouri* while we talked and suggested western chorus frogs, but the identification of these eggs remained unknown.

One late June day, several silver-dollar-sized filmy masses floated on the pond, each with two dozen or so minuscule dots. I tried to free an insect caught in one of those egg-laden filmy patches with a twig. Two eggs stuck to the stick, so I put them in a glass of pond water. A day later they were elongated and moved within the egg membrane, lurching into a curve and back. In profile they resembled tiny birds. I named one Tad and the other Pole. They traveled back and forth to Indianapolis in a Ball canning jar. After hatching, they grew on a diet of pond water, romaine lettuce, and the bacteria rotting the lettuce. By the 22nd of July, four weeks after his adoption, Tad's front legs had emerged. With four legs and a tail, he needed to be released. Next to the pond, he sat briefly on my extended finger in a statuesque frog stance, then hopped off and went back and forth between water and land. Pole swam away, his front legs not yet formed.

How did Tad and Pole become frogs? Frogs begin life as small, fish-like organisms with a long tail that serves as a swimming apparatus. They breathe through gills—lungs that develop early in their larval stage and help them attain buoyancy—and through their skin. They feed on the microscopic, slimy film of algae, bacteria, and fungi that grow on water plants and pond debris. A thyroid hormone stimulates changes. During a phase called prometamorphosis, buds near the rear end of the trunk emerge and develop into the jumping legs. When the hind legs are about the size of the animal's torso, the tadpole enters a stage of rapid changes called the metamorphic climax. Forelegs suddenly erupt through small openings in the covering of the gills; the mouth widens and develops powerful jaws and a large tongue; the lungs and skin complete their transformation; nostrils and a mechanism for pumping air develop; the gills and tail are resorbed by a process of self-digestion and thus disappear. Before the week of climax is over, the animal emerges, leaving life in the water as a vegetarian for life on land as a carnivore.

One June day, a wide, solid black band of massed tadpoles agitated the surface of the water along the shallow edge of the pond. Thousands of tiny creatures were ready to leave their aquatic abode to join the hundreds of tiny black froglets that leapt from the tremor of my massive feet. A few jumped back into the water and swam briefly, seemingly searching with alarm for floating islands of vegetation. Tadpoles in the water dispersed defensively from my giant shadow, but soon returned, jammed together again as though ready for a marathon race.

In late June a few tadpoles darted into the muck for protection when I moved toward them. I caught two in a kitchen sieve, slid them into water in a shallow plate, and examined them with a magnifying lens. I had read that if the abdomens are iridescent with a transparent covering over the viscera, as I noted, they would be southern leopard frogs. But had southern leopard frogs bred here? I wasn't sure. Another conundrum for me.

In late June and early July, the forest floor can be literally jumping with thousands and thousands of hopping, leaping froglets, each about three-eighths of an inch long. Stop and listen and you'll hear them in the leaf litter. A month later most frog calls have ceased, and the five-month breeding season for frogs in this region ends.

I am concerned about the large number of bullfrogs that first appeared in 2001. The previous year, 2000, there were none. Then the pond was drained, so that the dam could be reconstructed, and all aquatic life, including numerous largemouth bass, was removed. Fish were reintroduced, but not bass. Did the absence of bass explain the assemblage of bullfrogs followed by hundreds of bullfrog tadpoles? Could that single factor make the difference? Bullfrogs are serious predators. Bones of almost every type of vertebrate animal have been found in their stomachs—lizards, snakes, turtles, birds, rodents, fish, bats, and other frogs (including their own young).

Bullfrog populations are growing. In Indiana, bullfrogs, as well as green frogs, are classified as game animals, and a hunting or fishing license is required to collect them. "The season is from June 15 through April 30 and the daily bag limit is 25. They may be taken with gig or spear with a head not more than three inches in width and a single row of tines, long bow and arrow, club, hands alone or pole or land line with not more than one hook or artificial lure attached. Firearms used for frog hunting are restricted to a .22-caliber firearm loaded with bird shot only. Air rifles are prohibited. Frogs may not be sold."

While the number of bullfrogs is growing, the overall numbers of frog, toad, and salamander species are plunging and succumbing to change. Observations and scientific studies have sounded the alarm about amphibians, particularly frogs. What's wrong? Obviously, if you drain a wetland for development or agricultural use, the biota that called that place home are gone. The government requires those who destroy a wetland to compensate for that loss through either wetland mitigation (the construction of a new wetland somewhere else at a size ratio of 3:2) or wetland mitigation banking (payment into a giant wetland bank). However, according to Spencer Cortwright, Associate Professor in the Department of Biology at Indiana University Northwest, the new sites often are worthless for amphibians, especially the sedge meadows that are commonly constructed as mitigation banks, which virtually no amphibians use. Also, new sites are often far enough away that most amphibians, snakes, and turtles, which move at most one mile from their breeding ponds, cannot reach them.

Research published recently identified a myriad of possible other causes: altered rainfall patterns; weakened immune systems caused by exposure to pesticides (atrazine, malathion, and esfenvalerate) and subsequent parasite infections; increased exposure to ultraviolet radiation, which damages the embryo's genetic structure and transforms pesticides into chemicals that can interfere with normal development and cause birth defects. According to Cortwright, many deformities are natural, having to do with an aquatic life cycle. A worm parasite enters the food chain, where it breeds and lays eggs in a water snake. The worm eggs pass through the snake's gut, hatch in the water as first stage larvae, and enter snails. These larvae, now in their second stage, exit the snails and enter tadpoles at the point of their developing limbs, where fast-growing tissues provide an excellent food source. A water snake eats the tadpoles, hosting the worm parasite, and the cycle begins anew. Perhaps because water snakes have been "persecuted," mistaken for poisonous water moccasins, there are fewer now, and, consequently, an increased number of deformed tadpoles survive to maturity.

Given modern-day challenges to amphibians, I had my leaky old dam replaced in 2000 in order to support a healthier aquatic habitat. Constructed pond environments like mine, though far different from the natural wetlands that occurred in Brown County's wide stream valleys before their conversion to farmland, do support wetland species. Trying to establish a balance between amphibians, invertebrates, and introduced fish species in these ponds is a complex challenge, but an interesting one. The learning process goes on for me.

Some say that frogs are like the canaries carried into the mines of long ago. If the canaries died, that indicated the presence of toxic fumes, alerting miners to make a quick retreat. Do amphibian declines, disappearances, and deformities signal severe problems ahead for humans?

Declines have been precipitous in some places, especially where fish were introduced to formerly fishless sites, as in many California locales and elsewhere. In many regions, especially in the U.S. Midwest, the most severe declines took place in the first half of the twentieth century, and numbers have remained more or less stable since. Deformities in frogs are usually seen as limb malformations; they either have too few or too many limbs or limb segments. Less common are missing eyes or hind and front digits or split forelimbs. Malformed frogs have been seen throughout Indiana. To date I have seen none.

In the hope of arresting or reversing what some view as an alarming trend among frogs and other amphibians, the International Declining Amphibian Populations Task Force was formed. In 1994, at the IDAPTF meeting held at the Indiana Dunes, the North American Amphibian Monitoring Program was created. (Five years later, Indiana entered the monitoring program. I am now trained through them to be a citizen frog monitor.) The U.S. Coordinator of IDAPTF is Dr. Michael Lannoo. He states that it would be foolish to ignore or dismiss the message about environmental perturbation that malformed amphibians are sending. "Amphibian species will continue to decline until one of two things happen: 1) we exhibit the political (i.e., social) will to stop the causes of these losses, or 2) species become extinct." He believes that the future for amphibians does not look bright, although a lot of "nonscience (much of it nonsense)" is being propagated. "The public cares and a silent majority of scientists understand and practice the scientific method. And in this we take hope."

On my bookshelf resides the *National Audubon Society Field Guide to North American Reptiles and Amphibians*, a gift inscribed:

To Ruth Ann & Joe:

This is so you can recognize the amphibians.
Merry Christmas, 1995!

*Love, Clarence & Lois*

Clarence, my father, died on the 22nd of December that year at the age of 97. On Christmas Day we unwrapped the book. This field guide joined the other essential tools we need to lovingly learn about our frogs.

# Mycology 101

THEY'RE HANDSOME, muscular-looking, and tough. They're frag-ile, delicate, and spindly. They're velvety, glossy, and shaggy. They're abundant, singular, and rare. They're exquisite, stunning, breath-taking, and ugly. They're toxic and choice edible. They're opaque, gelatinous, and translucent. They're scarlet, gold, black, brown, purple, pink, cream, green, and blue. They glow in the dark. They're mushrooms, and they grow abundantly in Brown County.

Heavier than average rains and mild midsummer temperatures created perfect conditions for mushrooms in 1992. Unbeknownst to Joe and me, the beginning of a spectacular mycological show

awaited us as we followed the trail into the nature preserve a quar-
ter-mile up the road. It seemed like a routine hike that late July
afternoon. We skirted ephemeral pools where amphibians deposit
eggs in early spring, then stopped. We noticed numerous mushrooms on both sides of the path and wondered how many kinds
we'd seen since entering the woods a short time earlier. Twenty-five
or so, we estimated. Normally, we would have seen few to none on
this route. The circular hike that usually takes an hour and a half
took four hours that day. The presence of more than one hundred
mushroom species slowed our pace dramatically. Back at the cabin,
I called Lisa in Indianapolis. "You've got to come down and see
this spectacle." She was soon heading our way along with her friend
Xiaoling Xieu. What we found in our immediate environs boggled
our senses. By the end of the season, in mid-November, I estimated
that we had seen more than three hundred species.

In August 2003, while I was strolling near the cabin, I discovered
myriad familiar and unfamiliar species. It was a bittersweet morning, as I recalled Joe's excitement the day we had hiked through the
nature preserve eleven years earlier and felt my own excitement
over what I was seeing. Near the Pianogate was a cinnamon-col-
ored, suede-textured polypore with a cap six to seven inches wide.
It was so handsome that it took my breath. Beyond, a stump was
festooned with masses of one-inch-high orange mushrooms.

The experience with mushrooms reminds me of snorkeling. Gaze
across the watery surface of a coral reef, and the beauty beneath lies
hidden; but don a mask and glide along face down, and a new
world is revealed. Look into a typical forest with plant litter and
rotting wood covering the ground, and the potential panoply of

mushrooms may be undetected; enter under the right conditions, and you are rewarded with a magnificent array.

Fungi comprise a diverse group of both organisms and micro-organisms classified within their own kingdom, including molds, mildews, rusts, smuts (including corn smut, highly valued by gour-mands), slime mold—and mushrooms. Ancient Greeks believed that mushrooms came from Zeus's lightning because they appeared after rains and reproduced and grew inexplicably. The mycelium, a delicate thread-like structure that grows hidden in the ground or under tree bark, produces the mushroom or fruiting body that we see above ground. This visible part produces and disperses repro-ductive spores (similar to seeds). Spore dispersal mechanisms dif-fer. Some mushrooms, such as the highly prized morels, are spore shooters; some, such as boletes, are spore droppers; others, includ-ing giant puffballs, are spore containers. Thousands of millions of spores may be scattered and blown about by air currents before a mushroom is eaten or rots.

Living on both dead and live plant material or in symbiosis with higher plant forms such as trees (a relationship called mycorrhiza), mushrooms are among nature's recyclers, breaking down organic matter and exchanging nutrients. Without fungi, we would be walk-ing on thousands of feet of detritus in our forests rather than on thinner layers of actively decaying plant matter. The nutrients that mushrooms return to the earth help support new life.

In that amazing summer of 1992, Mother, legally blind by then, loaned me her Leica camera equipment, and my father instructed me on its use. "It's loaded with film," he told me. Joe joined me for our first excursion and the first twenty-four exposures, including a small, glossy green mushroom seen that time only. Unfortunately, my father had been mistaken. The camera was empty, and that round was a loss—a minor disappointment when compared to the dozens of species of fungi and the wide range of other wildlife I photographed during the following six years using Mother's camera, lenses, and bellows for macro work. Nature photography became my passion. Never mind the salty sweat streaming down my forehead and burning my eyes on sweltering summer days. What I saw through the camera's lenses added an invaluable dimension to our Brown County experience.

One mushroom was the stunning, solitary, and deadly *Amanita virosa*, commonly known as destroying angel. I gasped when I first saw one with its snow-white five-inch cap atop an eight-inch stalk, held at the base in its diagnostic egg-shaped cup. Across the creek, a cluster of nondescript little brown mushrooms, one to two inches tall, grew on a decaying log. The camera's macro-lens revealed that their caps were covered with shiny erect hairs, like minuscule transparent rice noodles; a tiny insect struggled in the stickiness of one. Some creatures are snatched by mushrooms, like that one, while others thrive in their company. After photographing a one-inch-wide mushroom, I looked into its hexagonal pores with a strong magnifying lens. Incredibly small larvae were nestled there. They were off-white and ten-segmented, with six legs, dark pinpoint eyes, and two dark, retractable, snail-like antennae. Brought into the cabin's warmth, two or three moved about in one pore and then busily climbed in and out.

While some wild creatures live *in* mushrooms, others dine on them. So do people. Say "mushroom" to some and their eyes light up, and out comes the word "Morels!" When young, I joined my mother and great-uncle Merle Robinson on morel mushroom hunts. We drove south from Indianapolis to a north-facing slope east of Martinsville. Uncle Merle knew where to look, and we always returned with a small paper bag full of our treasure. Back in our Crestview Avenue kitchen, a creepy-crawly occasionally lunged from the morels as Mother sautéed them in butter. Undeterred, I later hunted them near Geist Reservoir in Marion County, before the area succumbed to development.

When it comes to eating mushrooms, caution is strongly advised. Even the edible morel can be confused with the "false morel," though the latter is never deeply pitted or honeycombed like the true morel. If you collect mushrooms to eat, consider the advice of David Arora, author of *Mushrooms Demystified:* "When in doubt, throw it out!" Or Roger Phillips in *Mushrooms of North America,* who writes: "Keep one mushroom from any collection you eat in the refrigerator uncooked so that if you should develop any nasty symptoms you can give the evidence to a hospital."

I have collected and eaten several species of mushrooms from the surrounding area and did not identify all with absolute certainty. Under those circumstances, I kept a raw sample to test in case of illness. Anna Del Conte in *The Mushroom Book* writes:

1. Avoid picking any fungi that look slightly old, soggy, or eaten away by animals or insects.
2. Do not tear fungi from the ground or you will disturb the mycelium underground. This may disrupt formation of new fruitbodies. Dig up the entire mushroom with a knife.
3. Do not collect fungi in plastic bags; this provides an ideal environ-

ment for bacterial growth and increases the chance of food poisoning.

4. Do not put fungi that you cannot positively identify next to ones that you intend to eat.

She adds, "I used to be very daring and taste most species that I knew were not highly toxic. I've learned to be much more cautious since being ill after eating raw shaggy parasols. When you try wild mushrooms for the first time, always cook them and then eat only a small amount because you might be allergic to their proteins."

Do mushrooms have nutritional value? Generally their nutritive value is said to compare favorably to that of most vegetables. They are rich in the B vitamins, vitamin D, and vitamin K, and some are also high in vitamin A (e.g., chanterelles). Mushrooms are also rich in minerals such as iron and copper and various trace elements, and some types are high in protein. However, since some of this protein is indigestible, mushrooms are not a viable substitute for meat or other high-protein foods. Also, overcooking them removes some of their vitamins (and most of the flavor).

Mushrooms are known for other positive qualities as well. Dr. Kisaku Mori founded the Institute of Mushroom Research in Tokyo and is known as the "Father of Mushrooms" in Japan. His and others' research indicates that shiitake mushrooms, which are cultivated commercially in the United States, dramatically lower blood cholesterol and possess potent antitumor, antiviral, and antibiotic properties.

Identifying mushrooms can be difficult. Of those I've seen, many are not in any of my guidebooks. My growing interest in fungi led me to Whidbey Island in the Puget Sound, Washington, where I attended a course called Mycological Mysteries, offered by the North Cascades Institute. To help with the identification conundrum, my instructor there had the class begin with the spore print and its color, then move on to gills or lack of gills, habitat, size, and even taste and aroma. I made modest progress in this regard. The most conclusive method of identification, short of DNA testing, is to examine spores under a microscope. As a microbiologist, Joe was naturally adept with microscopes. Nevertheless, accustomed as he was to laboratory equipment, his antique one that we used here tested his patience. For me it was a new and exciting experience to see microscopic spores come into focus, giving us an opportunity to compare spore descriptions and field notes in our guidebooks to the real thing. For example, quilted green russula, *Russula virescens*, has spores that are "6–9 x 5–7 um [micrometers]. Warts broadly to bluntly convex; surface sometimes has short ridges." Fascinating and valuable information, but without Joe, the microscope has stayed in its case.

While most of the mushrooms that I watch for grow from spring into late fall, at least one apparently edible mushroom appeared here in January. A dead sapling in our scruffy early-growth north woods was adorned, top to bottom, with eruptions that looked like dark brown tree ears, which I added to a Chinese stir-fry. Then, in mid- to late April, morels, the most eagerly and competitively hunted of all, appear. I'm lucky to find more than two or three of them. The day Joe and I found our first, solitary morel was the same day we met a family whose ancestors had lived in the area. They shared with us their good news—that they had scouted the hillsides and valley earlier and gathered two bags full of morels.

That explained our one! In my best year, I found eight yellow morels, *Morchella esculenta*, and three half-free morels, *M. semilibera*. Since it was early afternoon, I left them in place, hoping they might enlarge a little. Also, I wanted Joe to share in the pleasure of picking them. At 5:30 in the afternoon, we bounded down the slope, an empty bag in hand, ready for the harvest. We were chagrined to find only two. The other nine? Snatched by morel-nappers.

Chanterelle, *Cantharellus cibarius*, is pale orange and vase-shaped with wavy margins along the upper edge and forked gill-like ridges descending the stalk. It has the scent of apricots when broken. We are warned to not confuse chanterelles with the poisonous jack-o'-lanterns, *Omphalotus olearius*. I think that they are distinctly different, but extreme caution is advised. Growing in midsummer, the chanterelle is my favorite edible mushroom—so far. Joe made potent chanterelle schnapps from our first harvest as I prepared a savory chanterelle herb omelet. *Russula virescens* is a mild, edible mushroom that grows about the same time and in the same general habitat as chanterelles and has a white cap with a distinctive green crackled "glazing" on the top. Chicken of the woods, *Laetiporus sulphureus*, is an orange and cream-colored shelf fungus, regarded as "choice edible"—the highest category used in reference to the edibility of mushrooms, signifying the most appealing flavor and texture. Harvested at an early stage, sliced thickly, breaded with flour and beaten egg, sautéed in olive oil and butter, and seasoned with salt and pepper as you would a fresh giant puffball, this mushroom is delicious, as I discovered after preparing and sampling one given to me by a mushroom connoisseur in Wisconsin and shared with a friend there.

Most recently I prepared, for the first time, *Suillus americanus*, which grew by the dozens under the white pine tree. They have slippery dandelion-yellow caps, which I sliced thinly and sautéed well in olive oil, butter, and salt. They had a spongy texture and a sharp, peppery taste—sharper than I'm accustomed to in a mushroom.

The edibility of fungi is more than equaled by their intrinsic nature. Stalks the width of a thread hold the miniature caps of a *Marasmius*. Mature puffballs belch gray smoke when raindrops fall upon them or they are squeezed. White, gelatinous, floppy fans ooze through cracks in decaying black bark of dead branches. Slime mold, like bright yellow scrambled eggs, snuggles amid emerald green moss on the stump of a once great oak. Teacup-sized earthstars, their powdery brown puffballs encircled by thick rays, muscle through hard-packed clay and gravel. An *Indigo lactarius* bleeds blue "milk." Coral-type fungi, the color of purple violets, jut from the scraped sides of an abandoned wagon road. A bright orange nipple, like a pimento in an olive, appears overnight on one of thirty-six small gray-brown puffballs, then recedes and disappears the second day. Raindrops cause the tiny "eggs" of one-quarter-inch-high bird's nest fungi to shoot out and release a slimy thread, enabling them to attach to vegetation. Pale, fan-shaped, luminescent *Panellus stipticus* grow unremarkably en masse on old logs, but when soaked with rain, they cast an eerie green glow in the dark. Want to know more? Ah, Mycology 201 awaits.

Mushrooms continue to lure me to faraway places, including the high elevations of the forested slopes of La Malinche in Txalcala, Mexico. In late August 2003, with sixteen fellow mushroomers, four

Mexican university mycologists, and two indigenous women, each with a placid babe held close to her body with a blanket, I joined the search for rare and not so rare, edible and non-edible mushrooms. Edible ones flavored and added texture to our tamales, soups, and scrambled eggs.

Locally, many call 1992 the Year of the Mushrooms. For me, 1992 marked the mushrooming of a new interest. Where will it lead me next?

# *I'm a Birder!*

*H*UNTING FOR *H*OPE by Scott Russell Sanders is about our crashing environment and the legacy this generation is leaving our children and theirs. The question is how to reach those who don't yet appreciate what's at stake. If only we all could awaken to the melodic calls of a phoebe or be absolutely still in the midst of nature's dawning cacophony. If only we all could watch a yellow-shafted flicker probe for ants in the lawn; a female towhee, the color of a cinnamon stick, scratch for tidbits, launching leaves into the air; a nuthatch deliver a husked seed to its mate waiting patiently on the trunk of a hickory tree; a bluebird hawk for a worm or hapless insect; a red-shouldered hawk glide through the forested

ravine, its banded tail spread wide, or perform its soul-stirring mating display with a thrilling "Kee-yer, Kee-yer, Kee-yer" as it flies up
and up, rides the wind, bends its wings backwards, and plummets
headfirst toward the earth; hear the songs of scarlet tanagers and
waterthrushes, back from their round-trip flights to Central and
South America.

One March evening, Sanders, who was writing *Hunting for Hope*
at the time, was a guest on a radio show called "Profile," produced
by WFIU-FM at Indiana University. During the hour-long program, they played a recording of a children's choir performing a
song about chimney swifts, written by Sanders's neighbor Malcolm
Dalgleish. The tangerine sun was setting, and the air was soft and
warm as I lounged on the deck and listened. A Carolina wren, bluebirds, a fox sparrow, towhees, a phoebe, a cardinal, chickadees, four
species of woodpeckers, nuthatches, and juncos came to my environment for nourishment; in turn, their presence nourished me.

Joe's sister, Mary Jane, sent us a *Washington Post* article titled "All
Atwitter." It distinguished between a birdwatcher, who watches birds,
and a birder, who may keep a life list of birds seen, subscribe to
*Birding* magazine, and find "the whole enterprise of looking for
birds to be extremely sporting." I am a birder.

Of all the elements that form the essence of this place, birds are
the most significant. I have written about those I've seen, heard, and
fed; their arrivals and departures; their calls and the time of year
and morning when they begin to sing; their deaths; and their mating, egg laying, and feeding of fledglings. If I were not a human,
my next choice has always been to be a bird. What freedom to have
wings to lift you unencumbered above the earth! And what views!

My mother loved wildlife, especially birds, and she passed that love to me. When I was a preschooler, she gave me a match-the-birds memory game, which is stacked, still, with my board games. She took me to National Audubon Society films presented on Sundays at the World War Memorial in downtown Indianapolis. I joined the local Audubon Society in the 1960s for bird hikes, followed my parents on photographic expeditions through the J. "Ding" Darling Sanctuary on Sanibel Island, Florida, and began to record birds seen in my yard, along the White River in Broad Ripple, and at state parks.

Why are more of us enamored with birds than with reptiles, fish, insects, arachnids, woodland mammals, or amphibians? For me, birds represent vitality. Although they may be hidden, mysterious, and challenging to spot, most are easily seen and recognized. Some sing melodious, bright, or haunting songs. Some perform amazing feats of strength and perseverance. Some display plumage with intricate designs, and others, brilliant colors.

According to Terry Tempest Williams, the author of *Red: Passion and Patience in the Desert,* the color of bird plumage is best described in Frank B. Smithe's *Naturalist's Color Guide,* based upon *Nomenclature of Colors . . . for Ornithologists* by Robert Ridgway and first published in 1886. I struggle to find the best words to relay colors and would appreciate access to Smithe's book. Reading about him in *Red,* I learned that *carmine* (described as rich crimson, bluish red, or the organic pigment produced from cochineal) is seen on a pileated woodpecker; *scarlet* on a cardinal; *flame scarlet* on a Baltimore oriole; *poppy red* on our red-winged blackbird and summer tanager.

Birds were in desperate straits one hundred years ago. According to Deborah Strom's *Birdwatching with American Women,* birding toward the end of the nineteenth century and well into the twentieth probably meant bird hunting—for ornamentation, sport, and food, including eggs. "The wilderness was dwindling and the birdlife of the continent, thought to be limitless, was in ruins. Extirpation threatened a host of species as a result of untrammeled hunting and the rapacious millinery trade. Feather hunters were known to slaughter entire nesting colonies of egrets, herons, pelicans, and terns to supply the demands of milliners in the USA and Europe." She writes about Frank Chapman, curator of birds at the American Museum of Natural History, who inventoried birds on the hats of New York's fashionable ladies in 1886. During two afternoon walks on the streets of lower Manhattan, he identified robins, bluebirds, scarlet tanagers, cedar waxwings, pileated woodpeckers, Baltimore orioles, and thirty-four other species. "In the end the anti-plume-hunting campaign was successful. Aided by the progressive conservation policies of Theodore Roosevelt and the Herculean lobbying efforts carried out by distinguished scientists and members of the National Audubon Society . . . birds were eventually protected and their slaughter for hats made illegal. . . . Stricter hunting laws were encouraged and implemented in many areas. The nature study movement was born of this battle." A century later, birdwatching, birding, and bird feeding are extraordinarily popular activities with a significant economic as well as positive environmental impact.

Humans still create lethal situations for birds. Habitat disturbance and loss, cellular towers, and window glass are some. Window glass acts like a mirror. What appears to be a normal land-

scape with earth, trees, and sky is instead a hard surface that damages beaks, breaks necks, and causes temporary unconsciousness or
confusion. Prior to 1998, birds rarely collided with my windows.
Then a larger window with inside screens replaced a smaller one
with an outside screen. The change was wonderful for me because I
could easily see the feeding area approximately ten feet away. However, with the new configuration, at least thirty birds hit the glass. I
documented six dead and seventeen survivors. Of those twenty-
three, seven were titmice. Others were goldfinches, a golden-crowned
kinglet, juncos, an indigo bunting, chickadees, a downy woodpecker,
a red-bellied woodpecker, a worm-eating warbler, a Kentucky warbler, and a magnolia warbler.

December 13, 2001, was gruesome. A titmouse whizzed around
the corner of the cabin and smashed into the west window while I
listened to Beethoven's "Eroica, Third Symphony." Whump. I threw
open the window and looked down. The bird was motionless. I
dashed out and picked it up. Cradling it against me, I came inside,
held it, and wept. Another flew directly into the hawk silhouette
pressed onto the window festooned with aluminum-coated cellophane strips that flutter and glitter in the slightest breeze. It flew to
a branch and away twenty minutes later. I moved the feeding post
further away, having read that, for safety's sake, feeders should be
mounted either on the house or more than twenty feet from windows. I didn't measure the distance and feared that it might still be
too close. Again, whump. Number three. Sprawled on the deck
with its wings outspread was a titmouse. I picked it up, cradled it
next to me in gloved hands, and brought it, too, inside for warmth.
Its heart pounded, but I couldn't imagine its survival. When it

squirmed, we went outside. It grasped my finger, so I placed it on a branch among the conifers. At first it held on, but its grip wasn't firm, and it tipped slowly downward. With it back in my hands, we waited until it could hold tightly to a small branch. Its equilibrium restored, it watched me for a few moments before flitting away.

One afternoon in early August 2003, an amazing array of birds, both typical and unusual, flitted in and out of the evergreens behind the cabin. Among them were ovenbirds and a worm-eating warbler, the first one I had seen all year. Two hours later it lay on the front deck on its back, fluttering its wings and turning in circles. I picked it up and gently turned it over onto its feet. It couldn't stand. A few minutes later it died in the forest, where I had placed it after cradling it in my hands and sobbing.

There are many suggestions about how to help birds avoid collisions. One thing that doesn't work, according to the National Wildlife Federation, is to close drapes and blinds with the intent of protecting the birds. Pulling drapes closed on the inside of a window will only enhance the reflection on the pane of the outside scene. I vowed to make this environment safer. I even considered eliminating feeders completely. However, now that the feeding station is thirty-five feet from the cabin and windows, the number of collisions between birds and glass has dropped to near zero and I am content.

On November 25, 1990, I listed in my journal the 10 bird species I had heard or seen during that visit. The number totaled 55 species when I created a chart the next June. The number now is over 120, including great blue herons and sandhill cranes, which merely fly over. I keep my data about birds on an Excel spreadsheet and print

a yearly report, now spanning thirteen years. Of the three introduced bird species that are ubiquitous in most urban and rural
areas—English sparrow (first noted in Indiana in 1876), starling
(first noted in 1919), and pigeon—I had not seen one at the cabin
until December 6, 2003. That black day the first pair of English
sparrows showed up, peering into bluebird houses and chirping
joyously; two months later, on February 9, the first starling landed
on the feeder. These sightings caused me to make last-minute revi-
sions in this manuscript.

In 1990, I couldn't have imagined seeing 120 species. Getting
there has been a struggle. Because of my work schedule, we could
stay for short weekends only back then. Nevertheless, I was determined to put appearance, songs, calls, behavior, and habitat together and make positive identifications. I was compulsive about
learning to recognize birds by their plumage and their calls. Now I
can identify the call or song of most species. Red-eyed vireos were
difficult. I had heard their nonstop, no-time-to-take-a-breath song
when camping and hiking in eastern forests. That same song drew
me deep into the woods across the road until I located its source.
Vireos sing in flight and while searching for worms and insects in
the trees. Their monotonous song is now familiar and identifiable.
Another "mystery bird" called with four rapid and moderately descending staccato notes like ones I had heard in the mountains of
West Virginia. In 1994 it approached, first to the edge of the forest
and then above me in the tulip tree. I held my breath and didn't
move a muscle for fear of frightening it. And then I knew: It was a
wood thrush! The bird with one of the most melodic and enchant-
ing songs has a call like the burst of a machine gun.

For years I tried to match a "cluck, cluck, cluck," which sometimes lasted several minutes, with its source. I concluded that it was
either a yellow-billed cuckoo (though no bird guide supported that
supposition) or a wild turkey (the same). In pursuit, I purchased a
book about turkeys and asked a biologist friend for the Florida
author's phone number should I fail to make a visual connection.
Years later I matched the sound to its maker—a chipmunk.

That failure aside, I hear "zee-zee-zee" and repeat it mentally. Is
a golden-crowned kinglet near? Yes, I see the tiny creature. I hear a
thrush calling, but is the call the "whit" of a migrating Swainson's
or the "chuck" of a hermit? How to be certain? Then it sings its
"soft breezy flutelike phrases, each phrase sliding upward," in Peterson's words. Yes, Swainson's. Shweeeeeeeep. Eerie, urgent calls of
whispered ascending sounds awakened me several July nights in the
predawn hours. What's out there? Then I found David Sibley's description in *The Sibley Guide to Birds* of the sound made by juvenile
barred owls: a "rising hiss—kssssshhip." Exactly. Three hung out
nearby. Their large forms coasted from the branch of an ancient
oak tree deep into the woods.

I have written hundreds of entries about birds in my journals
and faced the daunting task of sifting through them for the best to
include in this chapter. March 21, 2002, I turned on my computer
to begin writing the last of thirty-four essays—"Birds." Avoidance
overwhelmed my good intentions. I checked e-mail, paced the floor,
chased squirrels, looked up the meanings of words in *Webster's Un-
abridged Dictionary*, washed, dried, and put away dishes, brewed yerba
maté, and pondered the task ahead. Then it came to me: Condense
the highlights into a twelve-month time frame. If the format works,

I thought, the final stage of my final topic should be within sight when I next returned to write.

Our calendar year begins January 1, and that connotes true winter in Indiana. But for birds here, the winter season begins in November and continues into March. The weather is normally cold, sometimes frigid, and often snowy. The nurturers among us are compelled to feed our avian neighbors. Millions feed the birds, encouraged by articles with titles such as "Try 'Miracle Meal' for Bluebirds," "Bluebird Banquet," "Seed Preferences: East versus West," "Avian Cuisine," "Winter Bird Feeding," "Peanut Butter Delight," and "Guide to Gourmet Bird Feeding—Before you stock up on birdseed this winter, make sure you know what your guests really like to eat." Add to that "What to Plant for the Birds," "Creating a Garden for Birds," and "How to Hide a Berry Treasure Around Your Home."

When birds eat the peanuts, suet, black-oil sunflower seeds, thistle, and white millet that I offer, I'm happy. I feel the same kind of satisfaction after preparing a meal for friends who empty the serving bowls, clean their plates, rave about the cuisine, and leave the table pleasurably fed. Maybe I make the lives of birds a little easier. Maybe some birds survive because of my offering.

Thirty-five bird species have come to my feeders over the years. Sixteen of the twenty-three year-round bird species come: chickadees, cardinals, titmice, nuthatches, downy and red-bellied woodpeckers almost always; American goldfinches often; mourning doves, blue jays, rufous-sided towhees, Carolina wrens, and pileated and hairy woodpeckers occasionally; crows, flickers, and red-headed woodpeckers rarely. Once I bought a container of mealy worms (fifty at six cents apiece) for the bluebirds; the worms were soon devoured.

Hairy woodpeckers, larger versions of downy woodpeckers, come regularly to my feeders once they get started. But sometimes nine, ten, or eleven months pass without my seeing one. One day a novice showed up, checked out the procedure from the safety of a sturdy tree trunk, flew to the vertical pole from which three curved arms extend to hold feeders, and slid down. Meanwhile, inches away from the confused bird, downy and red-bellied woodpeckers flitted away with peanuts plucked from the peanut feeder.

Kit and George Harrison co-authored *The Birds of Winter,* in which they write about wildlife ecologist Margaret Clark Brittingham. She monitored 576 black-capped chickadees for three winters in Wisconsin and gave insight into how "little balls of fluff with bare feet withstand severe weather." Brittingham calculated that a chickadee needs at least twenty times more food in winter than in summer, must eat the equivalent of 150 sunflower seeds a day to stay alive in mild winter weather, and must find more than 250 sunflower seeds daily, the equivalent of sixty percent of its body weight, when the temperature drops to zero. Brittingham studied the survival rate of those with access to feeders and those without. "During normal winter weather, chickadees did not become dependent on feeder food. When people withheld seed from the birds, the chickadees survived at the same rate as those that never visited feeders."

The meadow stays unmowed during the winter to give wildlife some protection from the cold and to provide a food source. Particularly on frigid days, I enjoy watching goldfinches pluck purple coneflower seeds and juncos and American tree sparrows leap up to the heads of purple-top and Indian grass, ride them down for convenient plucking, and eat the seeds.

In March a noticeable shift occurs, and birds that migrated south for the winter begin to return. Chipping sparrows and Louisiana waterthrushes are among the first. During the last week of March, I bundle up, if necessary, predawn and drink my coffee outside, eagerly awaiting the waterthrush's first sweet song: "I'm back, I made it, so sweet," followed by a descending, jubilant jumble: "I'm so happy to find this wooded valley still here." If the waterthrush hasn't sung by the close of March, I worry. But invariably, by dawn on the first of April I hear that beautiful song echo through the valley, and my spirit soars. Was this same bird here last summer? Where has it been? What tells this little creature that this is a good place to mate and raise its young?

In April the number of species climbs rapidly to thirty, forty, and sometimes more than fifty (once I saw more than sixty in a week) when the warblers migrate through in May. That's a dizzying time when it's hard for me to stay focused on anything else. Waves of mixed bird flocks roll through the trees and stop for a quick bite in this fast-food parlor.

My two favorite summer residents are ruby-throated hummingbirds and whippoorwills. They arrive in April—hummingbirds often during the third week, and both always by the month's end. Both depart by September's end. Otherwise they are polar opposites.

Hummingbirds are magical, iridescent flights of fancy. Curious and fearless, these in-your-face birds hover in front of me and circle my head. I hold the feeder in my hand while they sip, and I feel the wind from the wings of these minute creatures weighing the equivalent of one and a half teaspoons liquid measure. Both speed and agility favor their survival. They winter in Central America, flying across the Gulf of Mexico. The ruby-throated hummingbirds, the only ones that breed in the eastern U.S., winter in Central America and fly each way across the Gulf of Mexico. They get their energy from floral nectar and protein from small insects, tiny worms, and spiders.

During their five-month stay, I prepare syrup for them with the recommended concentration of four parts water boiled with one part plain table sugar, cleaning the feeder every few days with hot water and a soft brush to prevent harmful fungal growth. (Red food coloring is not advised, since some commercial food coloring dyes may be carcinogenic.) If I count five in my general area at once, that is a banner day. In contrast, full-time residents down the road have hummingbirds that come en masse. Frankly, I questioned my neighbors' claim until I saw their birds, which swarmed like giant insects, vying for positions around each of several multi-port feeders. The nearest I have come to that was when the neighbors went away for vacation and allowed the feeders to become empty. A rare number of hummingbirds found their way to mine and stayed a few days.

Whippoorwills are nocturnal and feed on winged insects. Cautious, they are rarely seen. They lay their eggs on the ground and, according to Sibley, coordinate their nesting with the moon's cycle so that the eggs hatch as the moon waxes. This provides many hours of moonlight against which the adults can more easily spot prey to feed their young. If you value uninterrupted sleep, you might consider extreme measures to stop their incessant, repetitive "whip-poor-will" call. Once I got up in the middle of the night and shooed one away from a nearby tree.

In a name-calling contest, *our* whippoorwill would have left his competitors "eating his dust" the night he repeated his name more than ten thousand times. The first nonstop series lasted over an hour. He halted when a neighbor whizzed by in his pickup truck around 9:50 PM. Fifteen minutes later, another whippoorwill called in the distance. Our guy didn't tolerate that and began again. He continued past midnight. Whippoorwills repeat their calls once a second, more or less. One call times sixty seconds times sixty minutes times three hours equals 10,800 "whip-poor-wills." Frequently, two will vocally challenge each other; the syncopated rhythm that results is stirring.

I have had a few fleeting glimpses of their dark, horizontal forms in the dim light of dawn and dusk. Joe and I took advantage of their routine in late May 1995, when three or four began to call at 8:20 each evening. (The moment of the first call varies with the time of sunset, the last call with sunrise.) One whippoorwill began his calls in our neighbor's woods to the south, flew to the wooden frame of a decaying compost bin at the top of our meadow, and began his chant anew. Three successive nights Joe and I awaited him with chairs, blanket, flashlight, binoculars, and bug repellent. Unfailingly, he came. His body jerked with the exertion of each call. Occasionally he lifted himself into the air, fluttered to nab prey, swooped in a circle, returned to his roost, and burst again into song. Two of those nights a female silently appeared from the darkness and joined him. Together they flew to the next of six or seven stops. When the breeding season draws toward a close, their calls become infrequent and brief.

With the exception of parasitic brown-headed cowbirds, I appreciate all of the birds. As early as February, bluebirds and chickadees examine nest boxes and spar over their favorites of the moment. Bluebirds often dash my hopes when they select boxes out of sight or in my neighbor's yard. By the end of April, the first bluebird eggs are probably laid and ready to hatch. Carolina wrens and phoebes, too, may have hatchlings by then. Courtship rituals are ongoing.

Male blue jays, nuthatches, and cardinals (and others, perhaps) select seeds to carry to their intended mates and pass them from beak to beak. During this prenuptial month, chickadees gather nesting materials, including moss growing on the railroad ties and dog and cat fur. They plunge to the ground in fierce combat—beak to beak with claws locked. One day a blue-gray gnatcatcher flew to a dense web that filled the crotch between two small branches of a black cherry tree. Tent caterpillars crawled on the web's surface. Biological control of a noxious critter is about to happen, I thought. Wrong. The tiny bird pulled bits of sticky web into its mouth and flew off with this nesting material, leaving the worms unharmed. Bluebirds attack their own reflections (imagined adversaries) in the windows of my car. One time there were three at once, one on each of the two side mirrors and one on the roof. The most determined fluttered over and over to the top of my sloping front windshield and slid, pecking furiously at its reflection on its way down.

In May, bird songs fill the air from 4:30 AM to 8:00 PM. Cardinals, some of them with repertoires of up to ten songs, usually begin and end the day. One sang each of his melodies several times, and each was repeated by another in the distance. Cardinals sing romantically and seductively. Bud Starling, in *Enjoying Indiana Birds*, writes that cardinals may produce four broods a season, so they must be in a continual courting mood. One exhibited his mathematical prowess. His first song began with a melodic "dear, dear" followed by one "cheep." Again "dear, dear" with two "cheeps," then three, then three with a flourish, then two, then one.

Birding changes dramatically by mid-May. Most birds become indifferent to feeders, and seeds scattered on the railing are uneaten from one day to the next. I surmise that parents are feeding raw meat, such as insects, caterpillars, and worms, to their hatchlings. By June the feeders are busy again.

In late May, three juvenile phoebes, reared inches from my back door, exploded in unison from the nest for the first time and flew to the nearby trees. Their tails bobbed up and down, already true to their species. They had fledged before many migrant birds had even reached their northern nesting grounds.

In a good year, the worm or caterpillar population is dense, and tree leaves are riddled with holes, sometimes completely devoured. These worms make it possible for the baby birds to flourish, outgrow their nests, and learn how to survive in the big world. Nonetheless, the nest phase is full of perils, among which, in no order of magnitude, I name raccoons, opossums, cats (feral and domestic), black rat snakes, blue jays, crows, and brown-headed cowbirds. Parent birds must carefully choose a tree for their nest. Ground nesters, such as ovenbirds, choose a spot on the forest floor. With so many threats, I'm surprised that so many make it. Some species are at risk and endangered, but most are managing.

Bluebirds have made a comeback with massive human intervention. We have learned their box preferences and locations (best mounted above a pipe with the opening facing the northeast, according to Cornell University), established bluebird trails, figured out how to baffle snakes, raccoons, and cats and treat blowflies. Several boxes that Joe mounted have been successful. But most birds depend on natural settings, not boxes we provide.

There are many dangers for helpless birds. When I fell asleep on the evening of one May 9, there were four healthy baby robins tucked into a nest in an evergreen a few feet from our bedroom window. The next morning, the nest was in shambles with not a trace of babes. Then I remembered being partially awakened by vicious snarling sounds. Raccoons had raided the nest. Robins must also defend their nests from harassing blue jays. Another May, nests with four eggs tended by cardinals and three eggs tended by robins were destroyed during my three-day absence.

Birds use various methods to protect their progeny. Scarlet tanagers and worm-eating warblers feign injury, stumbling and fluttering on the ground to draw attention away from their nests. Some birds eject eggs laid in their nests by parasitic brown-headed cowbirds or build a second nest over the unwanted eggs. Birds instinctively recognize rat snakes as the threat they are. One day some cardinals, titmice, chickadees, chipping sparrows, nuthatches, indigo buntings, and downy woodpeckers sounded an alarm, darting in and out of a burning bush. The detested object was the horizontal form of a black rat snake stretched curvaceously across several branches. Unafraid, some birds perched a foot away from the snake, while others maintained a safer distance. But they all recognized this creature as fearsome. How do birds learn this?

According to Purdue professor Barny Dunning, the majority of small birds that hatch do not survive their initial summer. There are two major periods of mortality, and they occur very early: during the first nine days, when nestlings are killed by predators, and after the first three weeks, when starvation occurs after parents stop feeding fledglings. For those that survive those first few weeks, the average lifespan is one to three years, Dunning states, and they live to breed once or twice. For most species, the maximum longevity is often eight or ten or even more years. The champion Anna's hummingbird was eleven years old. These numbers, related to passerine longevity, are determined from banding encounters, about which Dunning edits a column.

Predatory birds may be prey for others. A flock of blue jays once sounded their alarm while I swam in the pond. A sharp-shinned hawk streaked over me with a jay clutched to its breast, another irate jay close behind. The hawk flew into the woods, stayed for a minute, and then flew away, still clinging to the doomed bird.

I had taken a walk in the woods at the end of May and followed the path along the east side of Cassie Creek, cutting across the alluvial plain where chanterelles grow abundantly most years. A brownish bird erupted from the ground in front of me and flew into shrubs twenty feet or so away. I focused my binoculars. I noted her heavily spotted breast and light buff-colored eye ring and pronounced her a wood thrush. I sensed that the bird was diverting me from a nest, so I proceeded cautiously. Was there a nest on the ground, I wondered? Then I saw an arch of brown grasses a few inches high. Over the arch and sloping away was green vegetation of the forest floor. I backed away and then looked with binoculars. This was a nest, and there were several eggs inside. Back at the cabin I checked "wood thrush" on my list and pulled out bird guides to confirm my assessment. Wrong. Wood thrushes are not ground nesters. I called Brown County resident Bill Zimmerman, the artist for *The Birds of Indiana*, at home and described the setting and nest. "Ovenbird," he exclaimed. I had made an uncommon discovery. I felt close to tears, realizing that with another step or two the camouflaged nest would have been crushed by my clunky boots. A week later the ovenbird dashed away from her nest as I approached. Through binoculars I checked the status of the eggs. There were two, white with brown specks. Fewer than before, it seemed. A week later the nest was empty. Hopefully the eggs had hatched and the young birds had fledged and had not become another creature's meal.

In June 2003, I wanted to verify my belief that it was an ovenbird I heard singing each evening for an hour at dusk. For some time I had thought about recording the song and playing it for a local expert's opinion. I didn't return with my tape recorder to the area near the dam until July 3. While storm clouds gathered and roiled above me, I waited for the ovenbird to begin. It didn't, again proving that I must take advantage of the moment. When I have a good idea, waiting may not work.

June is lively. Bird life abounds. Ravenous and demanding juveniles run their parents ragged. I've watched waterthrushes, titmice, chickadees, downy woodpeckers, vireos, indigo buntings, and more fill those gaping mouths. Many adult species come to the feeders continuously. The seeds, nuts, and suet that I provide may be as important to the bird population then as it is during those long winter months. Juvenile red-bellied woodpeckers love peanuts; they hang around in the trees near the peanut feeder and beg for more. They like sunflower seeds too. During one such feeding session, a parent pecked the juvenile perched atop a three-inch-diameter branch and forced it to the underside—a lesson on holding on tight while upside down. Nuthatch babes cavort in the trees, fat, sassy, and delighted with life, sounding like soft squeeze toys. I watched one day as some little nuthatches figured out a feeding system. They positioned themselves vertically on the rough bark of tulip poplar trees with their beaks pointing upward. The parent nuthatches landed above them, heads down, tucked the unhusked sunflower seeds into grooves in the bark, pecked off the husks, and dropped the morsels into the waiting babies' mouths.

Birding on my property slows down in July and August while the bird world coasts along. By then most eggs are hatched and broods fledged. Juveniles feed themselves and become independent. There was one notable exception. While meandering through the woods one day, I discovered an Acadian flycatcher nest with hatchlings. The nest was precisely as described in *Birds of Indiana:* "The small, untidy-looking nest is usually constructed from eight to twenty feet from the ground on a thin descending branch of a tree or shrub. . . . the usual clutch is three." On July 8, I led Joe to see the nest and its feathery contents. We arrived in time to see three fledglings clustered eight inches up the branch from the nest. One took its first flight of four feet to another branch; a second one followed. We quietly retreated.

While visiting family in California, I found the two-tiered shallow water fountain I had been looking for. Made of shale that would blend in with the stones surrounding my little patio, I thought it would be perfect for the birds to drink from and bathe in during the hot summer months. In addition, it would produce the trickling sound that birds can't resist. But in its first season, the fountain's only visitors were two slugs that hid in a crevice and a chipmunk. Once a goldfinch flew above it, hovered, and departed. Then, one day, I discovered why the birds were ignoring the new addition. In the valley, while resting on the trunk of a maple tree that had fallen across the creek and dangling my feet in a small pool, I watched as cardinals, chickadees, Louisiana warblers, gnatcatchers, and red-eyed vireos flew in and out of the encompassing trees. Then titmice and worm-eating warblers came for a cool bath in the seclusion of the shallow reservoir created behind the downed tree. It was no contest between my tiny manmade fountain and nature's creek.

July is evidently a good month for juvenile turkeys to take flight instruction. At first I thought my neighbor was hammering lightly and irregularly on a hollow box. Then the sound accelerated, and I recognized it as that of a wild turkey. I looked up into the oak trees that shade the space between my cabin and my neighbor's home. Seven fifteen-inch-tall turkeys were perched there, awaiting airworthiness training. Their mother flew across a narrow open space to another tree. Within a few minutes, all of her young ones had made it across too. They rested, and then she glided to the ground. One by one, the juveniles stepped into space and sailed down to join her.

In September, major shifts occur, one in my psyche. The hummingbirds and whippoorwills depart, and I miss them. For five months the hummingbirds allow me to be astonishingly close in a way no other birds do. But some of the best birdwatching occurs in September and October, when migrating birds stop to build their strength. Sassafras fruit is an important and tasty treat for thrushes, which, flycatcher-like, grab one on the wing. Non-migrant pileated woodpeckers, their feet suited for grasping tree trunks, thrash about on spindly sassafras branches, trying to maintain their balance while stretching for fruit. Occasionally they slip, and their wings and tail feathers become entangled among the leaves and small branches.

One day of birdwatching during fall migration can be so unlike the one before. The difference can be several sightings or few, several recognized calls or none, numerous birds feeding on sassafras fruit or none. With the trees still cloaked in leaves, you hope the bird you're following will appear from behind a leaf cluster so that you can identify it. The whir of wings goes by, its form unseen. A shadow passes over—perhaps a sharp-shinned or red-shouldered hawk or a turkey vulture or a crow. The migrants flit so quickly and quietly, and, absent songs, how can you identify them? Identity slips from reach; the expert birders are separated from us novices in the fall. You open bird guides and doubt creeps in. That yellowish bird has an eye ring, a pale lower mandible (I think), a yellow throat and breast, and a hint of dark eye line. Surely I'll find a matching illustration. I don't.

The natural environment provides the main sustenance for birds. Goldfinches pluck seeds from the dried flower heads of wild asters. Grosbeaks eat persimmons. Nuthatches ferret larvae from tree crevices. Sumac berries remain on the trees from one year to the next, providing a continual food source. One November my car was parked in its usual spot under some sumacs when dozens of elegantly plumaged cedar waxwings came to feast. They were on the hood, the roof, the side mirror, and the ground. I augment the natural with sunflower, white millet, and thistle seeds plus shelled peanuts and suet. Blue jays rarely come to the feeders, but when they do, they raucously broadcast their impending arrival, land with authority, and become the sole diners at the table.

A dark brown blob, which looked like a plastic trash bag snagged in a dogwood tree, moved deliberately. The blob was a turkey, which moved about gingerly for more than an hour in three dogwood trees, struggling to maintain its balance on the thin branches as it snatched the then black fruit. I have come full circle, back to November.

I could tell you about the bluebird in the woodstove, Tennessee warblers taking a communal bath, the prehistoric calls of sandhill cranes, why poison ivy is desirable, how you distinguish a male from a female pileated woodpecker by looking at their crests, and the emotions that red-tailed hawks evoke. There's so much more. This is merely a hint of what it's like to be a birder.

c carlson 04

# Plants Cursed and Cherished

TWO EIGHT-INCH FLOWER SPIKES grew at the far end of the valley meadow. Irregularly petaled white blossoms, about one-quarter inch long, appeared to spiral upward from the midpoint of the stem. Pulling out our limited collection of wildflower guides in 1991, we tentatively identified them as ladies'-tresses. Could it be? Wild orchids? Nearly positive, we marked them with red ribbon so that Grover would mow around them that September. They were the first wild orchids I had seen growing in Indiana. Since then, I've seen hundreds.

The Indiana Native Plant and Wildflower Society's main inaugural event in 1993 was a book signing and reception for the newly published *Orchids of Indiana*, written by Mike Homoya with photographs by Lee Casebere. Their book joined our growing natural history library, and we learned a fact from it that I've been proud to state often—that Indiana has forty-two native orchid species, more than the number of indigenous species in Hawaii. Aided by *Orchids of Indiana*, I have identified seven orchid species in these immediate environs. The first to bloom are showy orchis and yellow lady's-slipper orchids in early May, puttyroot and cranefly orchids in June, July, and August, twayblade orchid in July, and ladies'-tresses orchids in September and October. The seventh species I've found was coral-root, seen once in the fall under pines. Puttyroot and cranefly orchids have no leaves when in bloom. Following the bloom, the plant produces a highly visible single leaf that collects nutrients on through the winter. After seeing dozens of puttyroot orchid leaves, I finally discovered one in bloom in 2001.

Some of our native orchids are endangered. Because orchids, particularly lady's-slipper orchids, are exotic looking, it is tempting to dig them up and transplant them to our gardens. However, orchids have a symbiotic relationship with the ground in which they germinate and develop; therefore they probably won't survive the move. Horticulturalists are developing a way to propagate native orchids from seed. Nonetheless, beware if you see one for sale, and do question its source.

Indian pipe is another of our exotic plant species. I still catch my breath whenever I see one. Its shape resembles its name, and since it has no chlorophyll, it has no green parts. The white form is common, appearing in late July and early August. We saw ninety growing on the forest floor on July 21, 1995. Two clusters of a rare form, cotton candy pink, grew at the edge of an old log drag in 1992. From the time they began to push through the earth in early September until they matured and turned black in mid-October, I kept a photo journal of them.

Moving from the wild to the less wild, my "flower beds" are a mishmash of native and non-native species. My tolerance for natural occurrences is high. However, I did try to establish a showy perennial garden at the edge of the tiny patio. The first year it cheered me. Sadly, the introduced plants, such as astilbes, bleeding hearts, and hostas purchased from local nurseries, declined and disappeared within a few years. (I blame this on inadequate soil preparation on my part rather than plant quality.) The little garden had a mind of its own as stunning wild tiger lilies appeared and surged upward amid a ground cover of white violets.

There are plants in Brown County, and worldwide, that are infamously known as invasives. These are usually introduced plants that adapt spectacularly well to their new environments and aggressively out-compete locally adapted native plant communities. As they proliferate, they disrupt natural processes and can totally destroy indigenous wildlife. Nancy O'Connell wrote in the *Albany Times Union:* "Mother Nature has worked hard to provide us with an incredibly diversified world. Invasive plants begin the unraveling process of this neatly tied web."

Some invasives were introduced for seemingly valid but, in retrospect, unfortunate reasons. Crown vetch and kudzu are prime examples. Both were planted by highway departments to control erosion on bare slopes along road cuts. Crown vetch creates a Pepto-Bismol–pink mat when in bloom, but it fails to hold the soil in place as intended. It has escaped, and vast, dense fields of it now grow and bloom in midsummer along Indiana's SR 37 between Bloomington and Bedford. Kudzu, once thought to be a problem exclusively in the Deep South, where it engulfs entire buildings, now grows in Indiana, where it is monitored by the Department of Natural Resources and destroyed. Another cursed plant that was introduced by highway departments is the multiflora rose. The good news is that a natural fungus is infecting this thorny grabber, and the rose may die out from natural causes.

Amur bush honeysuckle, native to China, is an appealing garden plant. Its gracefully arching branches yield an abundance of red berries, which are liked by many birds. Both Amur honeysuckle and autumn olive were deliberately planted along Indiana's interstate highways in the early 1980s as part of a "Save Our Songbirds" campaign. Autumn olive now dominates far-flung old fields statewide, while Amur honeysuckle controls most woodlands in the Indianapolis area and other regions as well. Woodlands in Marion County, where Indianapolis is located, are now composed almost exclusively of old canopy trees and a dense Amur bush honeysuckle understory. I am alarmed to see growing numbers of both along Brown County's roadways, streams, and lowlands. Amur honeysuckle is particularly insidious. It has a long growing season and effectively shades out everything on the forest floor, leaving nothing but bare dirt. Some bush honeysuckles release chemicals into the soil that inhibit the germination and growth of other plants. The combination of dense shade and soil toxins means a significant reduction in the food and cover available to birds and other animals. If allowed to proliferate, Amur bush honeysuckle will destroy Brown County's forests and wildlife.

Purple loosestrife is a garden favorite, but it escaped cultivation and now clogs wetlands nationwide. It is considered such a dire threat to ecosystems that it cannot be sold legally in Indiana. Periwinkle's glossy, deep green leaves and blue flowers make it an attractive ground cover, but it is hard to stop. It covers massive portions of Yellowwood State Forest in Brown County. Costly efforts are under way to kill it. Extensive stands of Japanese honeysuckle vines cover fences, shrubs, trees, and roadsides in Brown County. These plants, woody and herbaceous, are weeds that will not halt their march into unsuspecting territory without human intervention, and that can be an expensive and time-consuming battle.

I tackle all of the above here, with the exception of purple loosestrife, and more. There is something exceptionally therapeutic about weeding, especially invasive weeds. I'm purging unwanted plants while protecting and promoting the ones I want to thrive. I'm doing something that can be physically taxing, and at the same is beneficial for the environment. I'm converting negative energy into positive. When I'm in one of my serious eradication modes, I ignore thorny branches and poison ivy, often ending up with my arms crisscrossed with scratches and splotched with poison ivy rash.

Invasives came to my Brown County property in various ways. Seeds of autumn olive and Amur honeysuckle shrubs were carried by birds, excreted, and germinated. Previous well-meaning owners planted periwinkle and burning bush. Joe planted dozens of clumps

of the ornamental grass *Miscanthus sinensis*, another introduced species from China, which flourished and provided a natural screen at
the top of our property along the road. It "escaped," however, and
hundreds of clumps, the product of windblown seeds, now grow
across the road on unmanaged property. I will need to be vigilant
for years to come, digging or applying herbicides to destroy strays
on my own property as well as on those others.

Native bittersweet is a symbol of autumn in Brown County.
Clusters of bright orange berries appear with pumpkins, persimmons, and ornamental corn at roadside markets. Some vines grow
to the upper branches of tall trees and hang their beguiling fruit
out of reach of those of us who might like to use them for decora-
tion. Others vine on old fences. (I wonder if our bittersweet has
been unsustainably harvested, as I seldom see it now in the wild.)
Nurseries offer an alternative, a rapid grower and prolific fruit pro-
ducer called Asian or Oriental bittersweet. Joe and I planted a male
and female non-native bittersweet, unaware then that, if untended,
it will escape and form massive thickets like those I've seen along
the Allegheny River in Pittsburgh. It too overruns natural vegetation and can quickly form pure stands in forests by strangling shrubs
and small trees, and can weaken mature trees by girdling the trunk
and weighting the crown. Oriental bittersweet may hybridize with
our American bittersweet, thus threatening the latter's genetic integrity.

Once we became aware of what we had, we dug it up and purchased what we thought were male and female American bittersweet plants from another Indianapolis nursery. Unfortunately, however, I later determined that they were mislabeled, and I have elimi-

nated them too. (I find that this is a common error. Nurseries continue to label the non-native species as native, both in Indianapolis
and in Bloomington.) American and Oriental bittersweet are nearly
impossible to differentiate in their early stages. Where the blossoms grow on plants and subsequently bear fruit is the telling factor. The blossoms and fruit of American bittersweet grow at the
tip of each stem; the blossoms and fruit of the invasive Oriental
species grow in the axils (where the leaves join the stem). I have
introduced vines grown from the seeds of the native species and
wish them well.

Brown County is known for its scenery. The gentle beauty of its
landscape has attracted artists and tourists for a century. Recently
it has become known for another reason, as well—its new, award-
winning public library. During these times when libraries nationwide are reducing services and closing their doors because of declining public funds, this county of fifteen thousand people built a
library that is fully staffed and open seven days a week. A wooded
ravine that runs along the eastern edge of the library's property is
viewed by thousands of residents and visitors from the building's
east-facing windows and the parking lot. The ravine had become
choked with invasive plants. A group of citizens, devoted to the
county's natural heritage, decided to make this ravine a model for
both public and private landowners. A committee formed, which I
happily agreed to chair. Its purpose is to educate the community at
large about our beautiful natural heritage, the threat that alien invasive plant species pose to the beauty of our natural environment,
the means of eradicating these alien invasive species, and ways to
protect our woodlands long-term. An offshoot is the Invasive Spe-

cies Assessment Project. This free service offers assessment of invasive species on individual properties and information about controlling them. It too is a model that can be copied anywhere.

Leaving the subject of weeds, I turn again to those plants that I love. Over the years, I have introduced many plants. One looks like a tropical exotic, but it's not. It's a green dragon, a woodland native related to the more familiar jack-in-the-pulpit. A bizarre Indiana spring wildflower, the green dragon produces a long, thin, tongue-like spadix, a fleshy spike that thrusts several inches straight up from the head. In the fall its large cluster of shiny green seeds turns glitzy nail-polish red. My green dragons symbolize the continuity Sanders applauds in *Hunting for Hope,* as the mother of my "dragons" grew three and four feet tall in the rich soil of my mother's Indianapolis garden. I planted one of hers under beech trees in my Indianapolis yard. It survives and produces seeds, some of which I collected and planted here near the cabin and in the forest. They thrive, and their fruit has fallen to the ground to produce more plants for me to cherish and to share with others. Continuity.

My records list more than two hundred species of herbaceous plants that bloom here. Most are native. Many were new to me. In my opinion, the most beautiful of these are common marsh pinks. If you see bouquets of pink flowers along southern Indiana roadsides in midsummer, pull over, stop, and take a close look. You too will become a *Sabatia angularia* devotee.

# Bittersweet

There is melancholy in the wind and
sorrow in the grass.

— CHARLES KURALT

FALL SWEEPS AWAY the hot months, and we glide into days that
bring sweet relief—sunny, dry, and around 70 degrees. Perfect.

To fall means to come down or drop freely under the influence
of gravity. With a slight breeze, acorns fall intermittently onto my
neighbor's porch roof and strike with sharp smacks, like dozens of
screen doors simultaneously banging shut. When chartreuse orbs
of black walnuts fall, some two and a half inches in diameter and
weighing more than one-fourth of a pound, beware. Featherweight
seeds fall, ready to germinate.

Foliage turns crimson and gold; seeds, nuts, and fruits mature.
Beech leaves are amber jewels against robin's egg–blue skies. Juncos
arrive on schedule in mid-October, and summer's avian residents
depart. Gentle breezes ripple the pond and create a kaleidoscopic,
impressionistic reflection.

With layers of brittle leaves on the ground, the minor rustling
of a squirrel may sound like a deer to my untutored ears, while the
cautiously placed hooves of a deer may sound like scampering squirrels. Masses of bumblebees, paper wasps, and soldier beetles feast
on goldenrod blossoms. Crab spiders snare insects with stealth,
while other spiders entrap yellow jackets and other prey in intricate
webs. Katydids jump from my blue-jeaned leg to plant stalks in the
golden meadow where crickets and red-legged grasshoppers leap
from stem to stem.

October can abruptly turn winterish. At 4:00 on a balmy afternoon, pileated woodpeckers, robins, bluebirds, kinglets, yellow-
rumped warblers, yellow-bellied sapsuckers, titmice, chickadees, and
goldfinches devoured sumac berries, insects, grubs, and seeds. It
was a feeding frenzy. The weather was still mild at 7:00, but change
was imminent. Thunder rumbled, and strong winds brought swirl-
ing, driving rain that commingled with leaves wrenched from their
tenuous hold. Rain and leaves pounded the roof like hailstones.
Two days later, the temperature dropped to freezing.

Fall carries us from sunny warmth to a more sobering, melancholy, and darker chill. On such a morning, after spending months
outdoors, except to sleep and prepare meals, I paced like a caged
animal from window to window with my hands wrapped around a

cup of hot coffee. The closed windows muted nature's sounds, and I felt less at one with the environment. My reaction to this shift surprised me. After all, I say proudly and defiantly that I really like winter, even prefer winter, in some ways, to hot, steamy, debilitating summer. Perhaps that cold and windy fall day symbolized the approach of the human winter that I am inexorably slipping into. Yet sunlight returned with radiantly golden air; puffs of white and lavender asters bloomed in the meadow and forest; and dogwoods displayed plump red berries against an impeccable blue sky. I shed my lackluster mood, telling myself that winters will be as good as I make them.

On a misty, gray 50 degree December afternoon, Joe and I hiked through the valley woods. We stopped to get a close look at a deep-sky-blue, shiny, ballooned mass the size of a blueberry in the wet leaf litter. Two snails were copulating. We knelt beside them with our knees pushing into the cool, damp soil and passed the magnifying lens back and forth for a close-up view of a slow-motion spectacle. These two hermaphroditic beings faced one another and moved near, swinging their heads to opposite sides. Sexual organs projected from indiscernible slits in the sides of their necks. They touched and connected, and the bright blue mass appeared. A slight disturbance from us caused the blue mass to fade to white before collapsing and retracting. Then, putting the urge to reproduce before alarm, they resumed with slow, cautious, tenuous gestures, exploring the space between them by extending their sensitive antennae tipped with dark knobs. If their antennae touched, their antennae shrank. When they had realigned themselves side by side, we stood up, straightened our aching bodies, and left them alone. Later, when speaking with Dave Gore on the phone, Joe asked him in mid-conversation, "Dave, have you seen snails copulate?" Dave's answer was negative. Afterwards, I told Joe that people must think we're the "odd couple." "No," he responded, "the perfect pair." Then, following a reference to chemical reagents, he concluded that our past failures had opened the way to our union, a major success.

All was not as well as it seemed, however. In 1992, the doctor expressed concern about the results of Joe's Prostate Specific Antigen test, a screening procedure for prostate cancer. The PSA rollercoaster began in earnest when, following a biopsy in 1995, a Sloan-Kettering Cancer Research Center oncologist declared that cancerous cells had escaped. Various treatments ensued. Two years later, we were still trying to be optimistic and live normally. In February, for the eleventh straight year, Joe competed in Bop to the Top, a race up thirty-seven floors of the American United Life building in Indianapolis that benefits Riley Hospital for Children. He made it in seventeen minutes, much slower than his previous runs of between nine and twelve minutes. Still, he won the prize as the oldest participant. That year, as in preceding ones, in order to get in shape for this race when the weather was inclement, he had jogged a looping path through our first-floor rooms in Indianapolis, counting to one thousand in French as he went, and concluded with a timed dash up two flights from the basement to the second floor.

A month and a half later, Joe's cancer was causing greater pain and was sapping more energy when I wrote these opening words for Volume VII of my journal beginning March 30, 1997:

❦

I am beginning this volume of my Brown County journal
with the certainty that before it ends, my Joe will be gone. My
eyes are brimming with tears. My hand feels leaden. My head
swims. I feel detached from my surroundings. But I intend to
keep the continuity of this record going. I would be unhappy
with myself if I did not.

Last night while I was watching the moon, clouds moved
between it and me. I thought of Joe and the cancer cloud that
is inevitably blocking Joe's light, and life. But I knew that the
moon, its essence, was still there, though hidden, just as Joe's
spirit will be here always. This Brown County place, as it now
is, is our creation. We have developed it and maintained it in
harmony with nature. Joe said to me the other evening, "This
is what I've lived for. This is where I want to be. This is ours."

———————————

Joe had been reading Carl Sagan's *Demon Haunted World* before
drifting into a nap in his new chair and footstool, which rocked
back and forth together. While he dozed, I went out. I leaned against
the east side of our cabin, protected from the raw wind, and imagined the silent world ahead of me without Joe. I scanned our
meadow, where chipping sparrows and titmice hopped about and
other birds scratched among the leaves beneath the evergreens.
Joe's resounding words came to me: "Isn't that great!" His boundless enthusiasm for life rippled through me and released my sobbing tears.

Chemotherapy was the next procedure—a series of five treatments ordered by his oncologist. (He tolerated only four.) The chemicals? "Poison," Joe called them. Despite Joe's best intentions, I began doing tasks that had been his. With Joe as my instructor, I used a caulk gun and electric drill to insert screws with washers through insulation into basement ceiling joists, tightened screws for a bolt in the closet ceiling, and mowed the grass. I wanted Joe to do as much as he felt he could handle, or even more than he should handle if he chose, but I wanted to facilitate and assist when needed.

We celebrated special and everyday events. We celebrated the news that Joe's children, Loring and Mary Edith, were coming from opposite coasts to visit; a long, nearly pain-free day with the aid of a single codeine tablet; the discovery of tree ears, a brown, ruffled jelly fungus, growing on a downed oak branch. (I added the tree ears to a stir-fry. Since we hadn't identified it absolutely, I joked, "Maybe we'll get to die together.") Bits of lumber, fragments of Styrofoam, chunks of concrete, stuff that he would have kept a few weeks earlier with his oft-repeated phrase "You never know when this might come in handy," were trucked away by Mr. Spicer, the refuse hauler. Victory over trash deserved a toast of Savory & James cream sherry, accompanied with Camembert and cheddar cheeses and French boule. Two successfully transplanted saplings? Golden sherry and 'Nilla wafers. Dozens of contrails crisscrossing the pale blue sky before dusk? Raise a toast.

For years, Joe and Cassie had hiked at least twice a day. But that now changed, and Cassie and I began doing the evening walks. Joe rarely succumbed to sadness during those months, but one evening, when we returned to where he was sitting in our favorite sunset-watching spot at the top of the drive, he was weeping. Canadian geese had flown overhead. "Almost prehistoric," he cried. This beauty would end for him.

Buoyed by painkillers, even in June he used every possible minute between sunup and sundown. He cut down brush for new paths through the woods and mounted a pair of high screws for the hammock above the other pair so that one could choose an exciting high swing or a low, relaxed one. "It's the period," he said, "the longer or shorter swing of a pendulum." We wielded an extended tree trimmer to cut down dead branches from the walnut and tulip trees. The environment looked so much better afterwards, Joe remarked.

In July, Joe suffered agonal pain, and his care was transferred to hospice in our Indianapolis home.

Several months earlier, on a November afternoon in 1996, I had found a radiant patch of scarlet and golden yellow waxy caps, genus *Hygrophorus*. Growing three inches tall among leaf litter, they glowed when backlit by the sun two-thirds of its way to the western horizon from the zenith. To photograph them, I hung the camera inside the tripod legs. From a prone position on the damp ground, I struggled to get the correct exposure and focus with my upside-down camera. Tree limbs cast intermittent shadows, but when glowing moments came, I snapped the shutter. The following spring, Joe encouraged me to enter the 13th Annual Limberlost Nature Photography Contest. After lengthy deliberation, we chose the scarlet waxy caps for the flora category and a crab spider with a bumblebee in its death grip for fauna. We titled the mushrooms *Aglow*.

Joe was not well enough to ride with me in late June to deliver my framed photos to the site of the competition, the art center in Portland, near the Indiana-Ohio border. His cancer was in its final, grim stage. I wept during that sad, lonely drive from Indianapolis across the flat countryside to deliver my entries. Weeks passed between that day and the reception and announcement of winners on August 16. Joe was sleeping when I left Indianapolis to attend. As I entered the art center, I looked to the room on my right and saw my mushroom photo. On it hung a blue ribbon. To my left, a red ribbon adorned my spider photo. I won first and second place in the only photo contest I have entered. The light was on in our room when I arrived back home around 10 PM. Joe was awake with Mary Edith, his daughter, by his side. When I told him the good news, he whooped jubilantly. Two and a half days later, he died with his hand in mine. The night of what would have been our eighth wedding anniversary celebration, a calling was held at our home for friends and family.

A memorial folder was assembled afterwards. Joe had ten nephews and nieces, all of whom remembered him for encouraging them to think for themselves and explore the world around them:

❧

"When I was about eight or nine years old, Uncle Joe came to visit us in Chicago. I had recently received a microscope for Christmas, and Uncle Joe brought an entire box of slides that he had prepared for me. (I still have both the slides and the microscope.) He had bone samples, blood, various germs, and other assorted microbiological wonders."

—*Jim Ingraham*

"Uncle Joe brought a tape recorder and recorded us talking and then played it back for us. I was only four or five years old at the time. At first I couldn't believe that I could sound like a different person to someone else, but Uncle Joe explained the different resonances of inner head hearing and atmospheric hearing. It was inadvertently a graphic early childhood lesson on different points of view."

—*Sue Logan*

"Almost two decades ago, while visiting Uncle Joe, I happened upon a giant glass jar filled with what I at first took to be stones or bird eggs, but their surfaces had a softer, fuzzier appearance. He explained that they were balls of dryer lint and that he was saving them up to measure the weight of the fabric loss over a period of time. I don't remember the specifics of the experiment, only his delight over the concept that technology had a diminishing effect on one's washables, vs. line drying. Many, many loads of laundry later, this still sets me to musing over how threadbare my clothes are undoubtedly becoming, but every single time I clean off the lint trap—every single time—I think of Uncle Joe, and now (hopefully) all of you will too."

—*Martha Logan*

---

In the awful months that followed, I would recall that photo, *Aglow,* and regard it as a symbol of my recovery. Somehow I would feel aglow again in Brown County.

Christy came with me my first time back to the cabin and helped
bridge the transition between my past and my future, but without
Joe I could see only endless empty pages. Gentle Joe was chemist,
microbiologist, immunologist, teacher, student, gardener, parent,
grandparent, creator, mentor, researcher, accumulator, tool user,
fixer-upper, ceramist, and wine connoisseur. He was my love, my
husband, my cheerleader, my teacher, my encyclopedia.

The next time I came alone, deliberately driving I-65 and SR-46
to avoid the back roads that Joe had loved. I gripped the steering
wheel hard as I drove up the hill to Lawson Ridge and to our gate.
Dully I settled in. Joe's gloves and drill remained on the shop table
where he had left them, awaiting his return. Then it rained, and
I looked forward to leaving. I wrote words, as I have done after
the deaths of all my loved ones, to Joe. *Joe, I know you expected me to
return, but how can I enjoy being here without you? I'm weeping. It was ours. So
much here is you—your designs, your creations. Perhaps that's the sweet and the
bitter.*

What could this place possibly mean? Nature and my observations? So what? I am not a botanist, ornithologist, entomologist,
herpetologist, or geologist; my observations seemed unimportant.

When the sky glowed bright copper at sunset that evening, I
tried to conjure what Joe would say to express his delight at such
beauty, but I failed. That impossible lapse made me weep. Then the
next morning, a bright, loud twittering drew me to the high window in the center room. Standing on my tiptoes, I could see a
Carolina wren dipping and turning on the handrail that Joe had
mounted by the steps. It cheered my morning.

Five weeks had passed since Joe's death. I was awake at 5:30 AM,
and it was still dark. I had no schedule, no chores, no social events,

no human contact planned that day. It was solely up to me. I got
up, curious about how it would go. I lit Joe's antique oil lamp and
edged past Cassie to the stove, still hot and with wood yet to burn.
I brewed coffee and, wrapped in a down comforter, sat outside to
listen. Owls, airplanes, and dogs. After breakfast I lost myself in a
good book and forgot where I was. Time passed. I turned on the
news and turned off the news, not caring about the most recent
multi-billion-dollar corporate buyout. Cassie took *me* for a walk,
and when I returned, I called my Indianapolis answering machine
and listened to the familiar and comforting voices of family members and friends.

The next month, on a late mid-October afternoon, as golden
sunlight streamed through the forest, Mary Edith, Loring, and I
scattered Joe's ashes. We each shared our words as well as writings
that we felt reflected his life and our love for him. After Joe's death,
I had found among his papers a poem in his handwriting copied
long ago onto a sheet of paper, tinted with age. The poem, "Death,"
was written by Hans Zinsser as he approached his death in 1940
and is included in his autobiography, *As I Remember Him: The Biography of R. S.* Zinsser, a bacteriologist, was a leader in combating ty-
phus and wrote textbooks on bacteriology and microbiology, books
that I found in Joe's library. I read this poem.

DEATH

Now is death merciful. He calls me hence
Gently, with friendly soothing of my fears
Of ugly age and feeble impotence
And cruel disintegration of slow years.
Nor does he leap upon me unaware
Like some wild beast that hungers for its prey,

But gives me kindly warning to prepare:
Before I go, to kiss your tears away.

How sweet the summer! And the autumn shone
Late warmth within our hearts as in the sky,
Ripening rich harvests that our love had sown.
How good that 'ere the winter comes, I die!
Then, ageless, in your heart I'll come to rest
Serene and proud, as when you love me best.

I had walked with Joe to his final moment and was prepared, as he was. Joe had helped me see life and death as a matter of chance. This understanding helped me accept his death, and I began to appreciate again what he and I had created here. I reread from *Sound of Silence* by Raymond Baughan, which was shared by Unitarian Reverend Bruce Clear at the memorial service for Joe.

Slowly receding surf,
tide going down.
A time ago
you taught my eyes to see.
And you are here
alive
within my memory.
No sliding world takes you.
You're here
as sure as sea
as sun.
I trust this slippery world
because of you.
We're time and tide
and life and love
and linked
with moving stars.

After unsettling moments forcing open the frozen driveway gates and priming the pump in the crawlspace, I unloaded the car and built a fire. Illumination came from the stove and a strand of colored Christmas lights nestled in a grapevine basket. Months later I wrote this to the host of public radio's "The Folk Sampler":

✺

Last August my husband, to whom I had been married for eight wonderful years, died of cancer. Seven years before that, in 1990, he and I had purchased a small cabin and ten acres of nature in the hills of Brown County, Indiana, as a retreat. It was a very special place for us. After Joe's death, it took a few months to enjoy coming here alone. Public radio programs from Bloomington, Indiana, have become an important part of my adjustment and transition. Saturday, the third of December, I arrived at the cabin from my home in Indianapolis just before dark on a cold night. I built a fire in the wood-burning stove and began to warm up while listening to "Prairie Home Companion." I alternately laughed and cried. Your program, "The Folk Sampler," followed. The theme was, "It's Cold Out There." I was wearing one of Joe's old sweaters and I started to dance. I danced for one hour to the music you played. It was an exquisite hour and I thank you for that.

———————————

Mike Flynn, the program's host, answered:

❦

Dear Ruth Ann, your letter is a bittersweet gift. I love the quick peek into your life . . . but it hurts, as well. My wife died about five years ago . . . and I remember how that feels. It took me a long time to feel that life could be fun again . . . but it is. A cabin with a wood stove sounds like a nice place to heal. Being able to dance is also a big part of regaining your mental balance, as well. That's what the music has to offer us . . . if we will just listen. I'm happy that you hear the music. Thank you for the nice letter. You make doing the program worthwhile.

———————————

(My e-mail inspired Flynn to create a program "dedicated to a listener to WFIU in Bloomington," entitled "Tripping the Light Fantastic." Christy and I listened for the first time to the tape of it, which he sent, while driving through an evergreen forest to the lip of Crater Lake, Oregon.)

The winter of 1998, I questioned what I should do with the dried peel of an orange. It wasn't an ordinary orange peel. If it had been, it wouldn't have shared display space with a hand-tooled splayed-wood bowl, a photo of a handsome flicker, the DNA chain bored into a Lucite column given to Joe circa 1980 for having one of the oldest Sorvall high-speed centrifuges, a wood plate from Ukraine, and other treasures. No, Joe had carefully removed this peel from an orange in a particular way. He had started at the top of the fruit and torn the skin downward several times. With the orange removed, he had an intact peel shaped like a flower with multiple petals. Only the flower was bowl-shaped, not flat. A-ha— the point. Joe had demonstrated to me how difficult it is to make a flat, two-dimensional map of our round Earth. I gently placed it outside to biodegrade, one of hundreds of bittersweet decisions that I had to make during those first months and years.

I couldn't count on my emotions. I felt elated when I drove down the drive in late March, expecting to hear spring peepers. I unloaded the car, put cold items in the refrigerator, and headed with Cassie to the dam to sit among the boisterous peepers. But rather than feeling elation from the sound of those thumbnail-sized affirmations of spring, I was overwhelmed by sadness. I wanted Joe to hear them too. But red and sugar maples and spring flowers were blooming, and I could write in my journal that I had enjoyed a good visit and didn't want to leave. I felt near to Joe's essence, and that was comforting and affirming.

In spring, dormancy ends and life reawakens. Spring peepers and chorus frogs sing. Days may be sunny and warm but with be-low-freezing nights. Then, sap flows. The landscape, washed in grays and browns, is lightly brushed with the pale rust of newly emerged maple seeds, chartreuse tulip poplar leaves, and scattered splashes of white serviceberry blossoms. Water rushes, drips, and flows. Buds fatten and flower. Daylight increases. Waterthrushes fill the air with sweet, clear notes. Toothwort, violet, and wintercress leaves deco-rate the forest floor, and green oozes through the pores of most trees. Amphibian egg masses float in ephemeral pools. You say, "Let's have lunch outside." You do, and golden daffodils dazzle your view while bluebirds go house hunting and sandhill cranes fly north overhead.

A minor twist of nature may bring frost and freeze, and occasionally snow, in April, and can wreak havoc. Daffodil stems bend and their blossoms wither. Bleeding hearts, which a few hours earlier grew green with flower buds, become a tiny, twisted mound of pale tan stems. Soon, however, sassafras, redbud, and dogwood trees bloom, and morel hunters comb the woods for a good harvest. Round-leaved ragworts and Virginia bluebells flower, and the air vibrates with swallowtail butterflies. Tulip poplars, cherries, and maples are fully leafed, while oaks unfurl their miniature leaves in shades of raspberry pink and silvery green; beech and persimmon leaves break from their protective shields.

A cool, wet day in May, noticeably greener than the previous one, seductively drew me from my journaling tasks. Rapidly unfolding leaves meant more worms, and more worms meant more birds. Catbirds, rose-breasted grosbeaks, Swainson's thrushes, ovenbirds, indigo buntings, and black-throated green warblers were eager. A worm-eating warbler perched briefly above me with a beak full of nesting material. As spring closes, summer and sweet life proceed.

Nature and life are bitter and sweet. From the bitter husk, sweet life has unfurled for me here, surrounded by nature's abundant variety. Here I taste a fresh new mushroom, see a new bird feast on meadow seeds, record the late evening call of an ovenbird, watch an orb spider create its web, and add a new butterfly species to my list. Here life, natural life, proceeds in ignorance of man's inhumanity to man, such as that of September 11, 2001. Here life has a refreshing focus and pace. Here sweet and bitter cohabitate. Life.

Joe, 1920–1997

# The Brown County Hills Project

I SUPPORT SEVERAL OF THE MANY outstanding organizations that work locally, nationally, and internationally to protect and improve our earth's environment. I was midway through writing this manuscript in the fall of 2002 when, as a member of the Indiana Chapter of the Nature Conservancy, I received my copy of their newsletter. An article titled "Brown County Hills Forest Block Project: Conservancy Helping to Protect Southern Indiana Forest" caught my attention. As I read the article, I realized that the intent of this project meshed perfectly with the subliminal message of my evolving book. Once I became acquainted with Dan Shaver, the project's director, and already being familiar with the Nature Conservancy's history, I decided that should my book be published, any revenues would benefit the Brown County Hills Project.

The valleys and steep hills in this area are the most popular destination in Indiana for outdoor recreation. Some estimate that more than a million visitors come here annually to hike, camp, canoe, fish, hunt, and enjoy the natural beauty and serenity of these heavily forested lands. These same woodlands also provide critical habitat for plants and animals. They are especially important for forest bird conservation, as the unbroken expanses of forest provide nurseries for birds that are in general decline throughout most of their ranges.

My property lies within this wooded expanse, a vital asset for the ongoing quality of Hoosier life. But because of the popularity of this region and its proximity to burgeoning urban areas, the pressure is on to develop and convert the private lands. The Nature Conservancy is committed to working with concerned individuals, private landowners, corporations, other non-profit organizations, and the government to seek a way to balance the needs of the environment and the needs of people. I am grateful for the extraordinary effort made by the Nature Conservancy and have been a contributor for many years.

If you want to know more, you can contact one of the following offices:

**Brown County Hills Project**
10 North Artist Drive, Unit 1
Nashville, Indiana 47448
812-988-0246

**Indiana Chapter of The Nature Conservancy**
1505 North Delaware Street
Indianapolis, IN 46202
317-951-8818
www.nature.org/indiana

# Bibliography

Aiken, George D. *Pioneering with Wildflowers*. Taftsville, Vt.: The Countryman Press, 1978.

Alvin, K. L., and K. A. Kershaw. *The Observer's Book of Lichens*. New York: Frederick Warne & Company, 1963.

Arora, David. *Mushrooms Demystified*. Berkeley: Ten Speed Press, 1986.

Behler, John L., and F. Wayne King. *National Audubon Society Field Guide to North American Reptiles and Amphibians*. New York: Alfred A. Knopf, 1995.

Berman, Bob. *Secrets of the Night Sky: The Most Amazing Things in the Universe You Can See with the Naked Eye*. New York: William Morrow and Company, 1995.

Borror, Donald J., and Richard E. White. *Peterson Field Guides: Insects*. Boston: Houghton Mifflin Company, 1970.

Boyd, Brian, and Robert Michael Pyle. *Nabokov's Butterflies*. Boston: Beacon Press, 2000.

Bristo, Alec. *The Sex Life of Plants*. New York: Holt Rinehart and Winston, 1978.

Brown, Lauren. *Grasses: An Identification Guide*. New York: Houghton Mifflin Company, 1979.

Burns, Max. *Cottage Water Systems*. Toronto: Cottage Life Books, 1993.

Burt, William Henry. *Peterson Field Guides: A Field Guide to the Mammals*. Boston: Houghton Mifflin Company, 1964.

Bustin, Dillon. *If You Don't Outdie Me: The Legacy of Brown County*. Bloomington: Indiana University Press, 1982.

Carmony, Donald F. *Indiana, 1816–1850: The Pioneer Era*. Indianapolis: Indiana Historical Bureau & Indiana Historical Society, 1998.

Carroll, David M. *The Year of the Turtle: A Natural History.* New York: St. Martin's Press, 1991.

Clausen, Jean. *To Thank a River.* Oregon, Wis.: Badger Books, 1996.

Deam, Charles C. *Grasses of Indiana.* Indianapolis: Department of Conservation, State of Indiana, 1929.

———. *Shrubs of Indiana.* Indianapolis: Department of Conservation, State of Indiana, 1924.

Durrell, Gerald. *A Practical Guide for the Amateur Naturalist.* New York: Alfred Knopf, 1988.

Elias, Thomas S., and Peter A. Dykeman. *Edible Wild Plants: A North American Field Guide.* New York: Sterling Publishing Company, 1990.

Flannery, Tim. *The Eternal Frontier: An Ecological History of North America and Its Peoples.* Melbourne: The Text Publishing Company, 2001.

Grooms, Steve. *The Cry of the Sandhill Crane.* Minocqua, Wis.: North Word Press, 1992.

Hallowell, Anne C., and Barbara G. Hallowell. *Fern Finder: A Guide to Native Ferns of Northeastern and Central North America.* Berkeley: Nature Study Guild, 1981.

Halpern, Sue. *Four Wings and a Prayer: Caught in the Mystery of the Monarch Butterfly.* New York: Vintage Books, 2002.

Harrison, Kit, and George H. Harrison. *The Birds of Winter.* New York: Random House, 1990.

Harstad, Carolyn. *Go Native!* Bloomington and Indianapolis: Indiana University Press, 1999.

Hartley, W. Douglas. *Otto Ping: Photographer of Brown County, Indiana, 1990–1940.* Indianapolis: Indiana Historical Society, 1994.

Heat-Moon, William Least. *PrairyErth.* Boston: Houghton Mifflin, 1991.

Hogan, Linda. *Solar Storms.* New York: Scribner, 1995.

Homoya, Michael A. *Orchids of Indiana.* Bloomington and Indianapolis: Indiana University Press, 1993.

Hubbell, Sue. *A Country Year: Living the Questions.* New York: Harper & Row, 1986.

———. *Broadsides from the Other Orders: A Book of Bugs.* New York: Random House, 1993.

Hutto, Joe. *Illumination in the Flatwoods: A Season with the Wild Turkey.* New York: The Lyons Press, 1995.

Jackson, Marion T. *The Natural Heritage of Indiana.* Bloomington and Indianapolis: Indiana University Press, 1997.

Katsaros, Peter. *Familiar Mushrooms: North America.* New York: Alfred A. Knopf, 1990.

———. *Illustrated Guide to Common Slime Molds.* Eureka, Calif.: Mad River Press, 1989.

Kaza, Stephanie. *The Attentive Heart: Conversations with Trees.* New York: Ballantine Books, 1993.

Kinsey, Joni. *Plain Pictures: Images of the American Prairie.* Washington, D.C.: Published for the University of Iowa Museum of Art by the Smithsonian Institution Press, 1996.

Klots, Alexander B., and Elsie B. Klots. *Living Insects of the World.* Garden City, N.Y.: Doubleday & Company, 1965.

Kriebel, Robert C. *Plain Ol' Charlie Deam: Pioneer Hoosier Botanist.* West Lafayette: Indiana Academy of Science/Purdue University Press, 1987.

Laessoe, Thomas; Anna Del Conte; and Gary Lincoff. *The Mushroom Book: How to Identify, Gather, and Cook Wild Mushrooms and Other Fungi.* New York: DK Publishing, 1996.

Lamott, Anne. *Bird by Bird: Some Instructions on Writing and Life.* New York: Random House, 1994.

Lannoo, Michael J. *Okoboji Wetlands: A Lesson in Natural History.* Iowa City: University of Iowa Press, 1996.

Lasky, Kathryn. *Sugaring Time.* New York: Aladdin Paperbacks, 1998.

Leopold, Aldo. *A Sand County Almanac and Sketches Here and There.* New York: Oxford University Press, 1949.

Lewis, Willee. *Snakes: An Anthology of Serpent Tales.* New York: M. Evans and Company, 2003.

Lincolff, Gary H. *The Audubon Society Field Guide to North American Mushrooms.* New York: Alfred A. Knopf, 1981.

Lindbergh, Anne Morrow. *Gift from the Sea.* New York: Vintage Books Edition, 1965.

Madson, John, and Frank Oberle. *Tall Grass Prairie.* Helena, Mont.: Nature Conservancy, Falcon Press, 1993.

Martin, Laura. *The Wildflower Meadow Book: A Gardener's Guide.* Chester, Conn.: The Globe Pequot Press, 1990.

Mathews, F. Schuyler. *Field Book of Wild Birds and Their Music.* Bedford, Mass.: Applewood Books, 2000. Orig. pub. 1904.

Matson, Tim. *Earth Ponds: The Country Pond Maker's Guide to Building, Maintenance and Restoration.* Woodstock, Vt.: Countryman Press, 1991.

Miller, Orson K., Jr. *Mushrooms of North America.* New York: E. P. Dutton & Company, 1972.

Minton, Sherman A., Jr. *Amphibians and Reptiles of Indiana.* Indianapolis: Indiana Academy of Science, 2001.

———. *Life, Love, and Reptiles: An Autobiography of Sherman A. Minton, Jr., M.D.* Malabar, Fla.: Krieger Publishing Company, 2001.

Mumford, Russell E., and Charles E. Keller. *The Birds of Indiana.* Bloomington: Indiana University Press, 1984.

Nelson, Richard. *Heart and Blood: Living with Deer in America.* New York: Alfred A. Knopf, 1997.

Newcomb, Lawrence. *Newcomb's Wildflower Guide.* Boston, Toronto, and London: Little, Brown and Company, 1977.

Niering, William A., and Nancy C. Olmstead. *The Audubon Society Field Guide to North American Wildflowers: Eastern Region.* New York: Alfred A. Knopf, 1979.

O'Connell, Nancy. "Invasive Plants Tangle with Mother Nature." *Albany Times Union,* November 3, 2002, Section H, p. 1.

O'Connor, Patricia T. *Words Fail Me: What Everyone Who Writes Should Know about Writing.* Orlando, Fla.: Harcourt, 1999.

Oliver, Mary. *New and Selected Poems.* Boston: Beacon Press, 1992.

Patterson, Freeman. *Photography and the Art of Seeing.* New York: Van Nostrand Reinhold, 1979.

Penner, Mil, and Carol Schmidt. *Prairie: The Land and Its People.* Inman, Kans.: Sounds of Kansas, 1989.

Peterson, Roger Tory. *Peterson Field Guides: Eastern Birds.* Boston: Houghton Mifflin, 1980.

Petrides, George A. *Peterson Field Guides: A Field Guide to Trees and Shrubs.* Boston: Houghton Mifflin Company, 1972.

Phillips, Kathryn. *Tracing the Vanishing Frogs: An Ecological Mystery.* New York: Penguin Books, 1994.

Phillips, Roger. *Mushrooms of North America.* Boston: Little, Brown and Company, 1991.

——. *Wild Food.* Boston and Toronto: Little, Brown and Company, 1986.

Plum, Sydney Landon. *Coming through the Swamp: The Nature Writings of Gene Stratton Porter.* Salt Lake City: University of Utah Press, 1996.

Pollan, Michael. *Second Nature: A Gardener's Education.* New York: The Atlantic Monthly Press, 1991.

Powning, Beth. *Home: Chronicle of a North Country Life.* New York: Stewart, Tabori & Chang, 1996.

Preston-Mafham, Ken. *Grasshoppers and Mantids of the World.* New York: Facts on File, 1990.

Pringle, Laurence. *Wild Foods: A Beginner's Guide to Identifying, Harvesting and Cooking Safe and Tasty Plants from the Outdoors.* New York: Four Winds Press, 1978.

Puleston, Dennis. *A Nature Journal: A Naturalist's Year on Long Island.* New York and London: W. W. Norton & Company, 1992.

Pyle, Robert Michael. *Chasing Monarchs: Migrating with the Butterflies of Passage.* New York: Houghton Mifflin Company, 1999.

Reader's Digest. *Our Magnificent Wildlife: How to Enjoy and Preserve It.* Pleasantville, N.Y.: The Reader's Digest Association, 1975.

Robbins, Chandler; Bertel Bruun; and Herbert Zim. *Birds of North America.* New York: Golden Press, 1983.

Rosen, Judge Samuel R. *A Judge Judges Mushrooms*. Nashville, Ind.: Highlander Press, 1982.

Sanders, Scott Russell. *Hunting for Hope: A Father's Journeys*. Boston: Beacon Press, 1998.

———. *Writing from the Center*. Bloomington and Indianapolis: Indiana University Press, 1995.

Schaaf, Fred. *Seeing the Sky: 100 Projects, Activities and Explorations in Astronomy*. New York: John Wiley & Sons, 1990.

Shull, Ernest M. *The Butterflies of Indiana*. Bloomington and Indianapolis: Indiana Academy of Science, 1987.

Sibley, David Allen. *The Sibley Guide to Bird Life and Behavior*. New York: Alfred Knopf, 2001.

———. *The Sibley Guide to Birds*. New York: Alfred Knopf, 2000.

Sieber, Ellen, and Cheryl Ann Munson. *Looking at History: Indiana's Hoosier National Forest Region, 1600 to 1950*. Bloomington and Indianapolis: Indiana University Press, 1994.

Skutch, Alexander. *The Life of the Hummingbird*. New York: Crown Publishers, 1973.

Smith, Alexander H. *The Mushroom Hunter's Field Guide*. Ann Arbor: University of Michigan Press, 1963.

Starling, Alfred (Bud). *Enjoying Indiana Birds*. Bloomington and London: Indiana University Press, 1978.

Steele, Selma N.; Theodore L Steele; and Wilbur David Peat. *The House of the Singing Winds: The Life and Work of T. C. Steele*. Indianapolis: Indiana Historical Society, 1966, 1990.

Stein, Sara. *Noah's Garden: Restoring the Ecology of Our Own Back Yards*. Boston and New York: Houghton Mifflin, 1993.

Stratton-Porter, Gene. "Tales You Won't Believe." *Good Housekeeping*, January and February 1924.

Strom, Deborah. *Birdwatching with American Women: A Selection of Nature Writings*. New York and London: W. W. Norton, 1986.

Symonds, George W. D. *The Tree Identification Book.* New York: Quill, 1958.

Thoreau, Henry D. *Faith in a Seed: The Dispersion of Seeds and Other Natural History Writings.* Washington, D.C.: Island Press/Shearwater Books, 1993.

Tjernagel, Peder Gustav. *The Follinglo Dog Book: A Norwegian Pioneer Story from Iowa.* Iowa City: University of Iowa Press, 1999.

Trimble, Stephen. *Words from the Land: Encounters with Natural History Writing.* Salt Lake City: Gibbs M. Smith, 1988.

Urquhart, F. A. *The Monarch Butterfly.* Toronto: University of Toronto Press, 1960.

Van Matre, Steve, and Bill Weiler. *The Earth Speaks: An Acclimatization Journal.* Warrenville, Ill.: The Institute for Earth Education, 1991.

Wampler, Maryrose, and Fred Wampler. *Wildflowers of Indiana.* Bloomington and Indianapolis: Indiana University Press, 1988.

Williams, Terry Tempest. *Red: Passion and Patience in the Desert.* New York: Random House, 2002.

Wilson, Edward O. *The Diversity of Life.* Cambridge, Mass.: The Belknap Press of Harvard University Press, 1992.

——. *Naturalist.* Washington, D.C.: Island Press/Shearwater Books, 1994.

Wilson, Jim. *Landscaping with Wildflowers.* Boston: Houghton Mifflin Company, 1992.

Wright, Amy Bartlett. *Peterson First Guides: Caterpillars—A Simplified Field Guide to the Caterpillars of Common Butterflies and Moths of North America.* Boston: Houghton Mifflin, 1993.

Xerces Society/Smithsonian Institution. *Butterfly Gardening: Creating Summer Magic in Your Garden.* San Francisco: Sierra Club Books, 1990.

Yatskievych, Kay. *Field Guide to Indiana Wildflowers.* Bloomington and Indianapolis: Indiana University Press, 2000.

Zinsser, Hans. *As I Remember Him: The Biography of R. S.* Boston: Little, Brown and Company, 1940.

Zwinger, Ann Haymond. *Shaped by Wind and Water: Reflections of a Naturalist.* Minneapolis: Milkweed Editions, 2000.

Lifetime Hoosier and Purdue graduate Ruth Ann Ingraham
is a traveler, naturalist, mother of two daughters, and volunteer.
While in the criminal justice field, she helped to establish a
correctional aftercare network. A co-founder of the Indiana
Native Plant and Wildflower Society (INPAWS), she now divides
her time between Indianapolis and Brown County, Indiana.

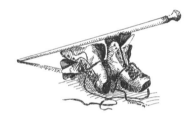

Photographs by Ruth Ann Ingraham
Line drawings by Christine N. Carlson of Creative Ink, Indianapolis